Subconscious Mind

The Essential Guide To Reprogram Your Mind

(Practical Techniques To Unleash The Power Of Your Subconscious Mind)

Sean Ammons

Published By **Elena Holly**

Sean Ammons

All Rights Reserved

Subconscious Mind: The Essential Guide To Reprogram Your Mind (Practical Techniques To Unleash The Power Of Your Subconscious Mind)

ISBN 978-1-77485-641-3

All rights reserved. No part of this guidebook shall be reproduced in any form without permission in writing from the publisher except in the case of brief quotations embodied in critical articles or reviews.

Legal & Disclaimer

The information contained in this ebook is not designed to replace or take the place of any form of medicine or professional medical advice. The information in this ebook has been provided for educational & entertainment purposes only.

The information contained in this book has been compiled from sources deemed reliable, and it is accurate to the best of the Author's knowledge; however, the Author cannot guarantee its accuracy and validity and cannot be held liable for any errors or omissions. Changes are periodically made to this book. You must consult your doctor or get professional medical advice before using any of the suggested remedies, techniques, or information in this book.

Upon using the information contained in this book, you agree to hold harmless the Author from and against any damages, costs, and expenses, including any legal fees potentially resulting from the application of any of the information provided by this guide. This disclaimer applies to any damages or injury caused by the use and application, whether directly or indirectly, of any advice or information presented, whether for breach of contract, tort, negligence, personal injury, criminal intent, or under any other cause of action.

You agree to accept all risks of using the information presented inside this book. You need to consult a professional medical practitioner in order to ensure you are both able and healthy enough to participate in this program.

TABLE OF CONTENTS

Introduction 1

Chapter 1: What Is Mind Control? 3

Chapter 2: How Does Mind Control Work? 12

Chapter 3: What Are The Benefits Of Using Mind Control? 21

Chapter 4: Beginners Techniques 31

Chapter 5: Advanced Techniques 41

Chapter 6: Techniques For Career & Success 51

Chapter 7: 7 Emotions That Harm You ... 57

Chapter 8: 7 Attitudes That Block Abundance 81

Chapter 9: Ask Your Subconscious 89

Chapter 10: How To Reprogram Your Subconscious Mind 93

Chapter 11: The Structure 98

Chapter 12: What's With The Subconscious Mind? 115

Chapter 13: Connect With Your Subconscious Mind 123

Chapter 14: How To Make The Subconscious Mind Work For You........ 132

Chapter 15: How To Tell If Someone Is Using Mind Control On You................... 147

Chapter 16: Warnings About Using Mind Control... 158

Chapter 17: The Difference Between The Conscious And Subconscious Mind 164

Chapter 18: Techniques For Health 170

Chapter 19: Techniques For Wealth 175

Chapter 20: Techniques For Relationships 179

Conclusion 183

Introduction

I am writing this book to introduce the idea of mind control to everyone. I want people to understand that it really is possible to use mind control on those around you and it is possible for those around you to use mind control on you. I am writing this because I want those who are using mind control to understand how it really works and for those who are being controlled to understand that they can break free of mind control. There are benefits to using mind control and I will discuss them in this book. If you are interested in using mind control, I feel that it is very important for you to have the best information available.

With that in mind, I spent days searching for as much information as I could find to pass on to you the reader about using mind control. Please be forewarned using mind control on anyone is not a game, it is very serious and should be treated as such. Please read through the entire eBook before attempting any form of mind control. You will learn what mind control is, how it works and how to use it in your everyday life.

You will also learn how you can benefit from learning how to use mind control as well as how to know if someone is using mind control techniques on you. There are warnings in the final chapter that you must know before trying to perform mind control.

CHAPTER 1: What is Mind Control?

Mind control is the method used to control the mind of a human and influence control over the actions of said person. Mind control is also referred to as brain washing, thought control, coercive persuasion. It results in the inability to think independently or have any control over behavior, emotions, and actions. Many people think that mind control is when a person uses cunning methods to coerce others to conform to the wishes of the one who is manipulating them. Although using cunning methods is part of using mind control, it does not always have to be about manipulation. People also perceive mind control as something that is bad and is only used by bad people. This is another false perception. Mind control is only bad if it takes advantage of the person it is being used on, but the fact is that you cannot make someone do something that they are morally or ethically against doing. For instance, you cannot make someone who believes that murder is wrong commit murder. Mind control can be used to bring out the worst in people as well as the best in people, it all depends on the person who controlling the mind of someone.

Thought reform is actually learning how to change people's minds and behaviors. Influencing the way people think is not negative. All of us influence the way people think on a daily basis, using mind control is simply taking control of that influence and using it for your own benefit. When you watch television ads you are being subjected to coercive persuasion you told multiple times how happy the product on television will make you and how you must have it. Those who are easily coerced are convinced that they cannot live without the product advertised on the television. Think about it like this, has your child ever been watching television and an ad come on of the newest toy available? While watching the ad the child becomes almost hypnotized by it and when it is over the child is convinced that they must have the toy!

They will tell you that they won't have any friends if you don't buy it for them or they will never be happy without that particular toy. Coercive persuasion has been used on them. It was not unethical nor was it someone trying to manipulate the child in a negative way, it was simply and ad that was trying to sell a product.

Mind control is not about turning people into zombies to do what you wish at your will, it is simply about influencing the way they think in order to get what you want.

Today, mind control has nothing to do with magic powers or mysterious arts, it is simply about marketing. Many people are put off by the thought of mind control, thinking that it causes people to do crazy things but the fact is that the everyday person can use coercive persuasion to alter someone's thoughts and get them to do what they want.

Mind control has been used by many governments on its citizens for things such as terrorist attacks, assassinations, and mass shootings just to name a few but that kind of mind control takes years to learn and it is done by way of torture, electric impulses, strict regimes, and many other unethical practices. That is not the type of mind control that you can use in your life on a daily basis.

There also have been cases where using certain drugs or heavily medicating a person can enable someone to control the mind of another. Physical, emotional, and mental abuse are also forms of mind control. Have you ever known a woman who was suffering from physical, emotional, or mental abuse? Have you noticed that she will jump at the chance to make here partner happy? Even though she is being tormented, and tortured, she does everything she can to try and do better. This technique of mind control being used is a very popular one. It is where the person manipulating will withhold love from the one who is being manipulated. They may also physically torture the person causing a mental break. The person they are manipulating will become reliant on them to make all of their decisions for them and they will do anything to receive any form of love from the manipulator.

That is not the type of mind control you will learn in this book. For this book we are going to stick to controlling the mind of others through influence and getting what you want through persuasive coercion. There is no need to torture someone in order for you to get them to do what you want them to do.

Who Can You Use Mind Control On?

The short answer is anyone is susceptible to mind control, but there are those who are more vulnerable than others. Here is a list of traits that make people more vulnerable to mind control.

✓ Those who do not understand how mind control works,

✓ Those who have the mentality that "it will never happen to me",

✓ Those who think everyone is basically good,

✓ Those who do not want to believe that there are evil people in this world.,

✓ Those who have low self-esteem,

✓ Those who are facing a stressful situation such as the loss of a job or relationship,

✓ Those who feel alone,

✓ Those who are dissatisfied with life,

✓ Those who have the desire to take care of others,

✓ Those who have a high regard for authority,

✓ Those who are seeking spirituality,

✓ Those who are suffering from some form of anxiety or depression,

✓ Those who are addicted to drugs or alcohol,

✓ Those who are preoccupied with what others think about them.

There are there factors that will matter when you are trying to learn and use mind control. The first factor is called your private personality, this is who you truly are. Your thoughts, feelings, hopes, and values. These may be things that you do not share with those around you. The second factor is your public self, this is how you behave around people, this is what you share with those around you. It is usually your most positive features. Finally your reputation will be the last factor that will play a part in your ability to use mind control. If you are perceived as a person who cannot be trusted or a person that others do not feel comfortable around than you will not be able to use mind control on those around you. On the other hand, if you are perceived as someone who is very trust worthy and everyone is able to relax when they are around you, mind control will be very easy for you.

Mind control is all about power. It is about having the power over others in order to get them to do what you want them to do. It does not matter if it is getting them to give you a big raise or if you are trying to get them to buy your product, it is all about having the power over their mind in order to get them to do so.

Many people think that parents use mind control on their children when they are trying to raise them with social, moral, cultural and personal standards. They feel that in a way the parents are influencing the child's mind to become exactly what the parents want them to be. It is also a common belief that the military uses mind control on its recruits when they are submitted to techniques that belittle or demoralize them in order to break down their personal ego and build up the idea of group identification.

Many also believe that when a person is taken captive and they begin to feel compassion for their captor that they are a victim of mind control. Some people also believe that subliminal messages in television ads and programming is a form of mind control.

In Haiti, people are made into living zombies and forced to work as slaves on farms given drugs that allow their master to use mind control on them. Very few of these people ever rebel against their masters and even fewer ever escape their bondage.

In this book, I simply want to discuss the types of mind control you can use on a daily basis in order to get what you want from those around you. When it comes to the ethics of mind control, it is up to each individual person to determine how far they will take using mind control and if the benefits outweigh the risks.

CHAPTER 2: How Does Mind Control Work?

When you use mind control on a person, they are not even aware of what is happening, and when they reach a decision, they think they have done it completely of their own free will. They have actually reached the decision on their own, but with the help of your influence.

When you master mind control, you will be able to influence those around you, plant seeds of suggestion in their minds, and get them to do what you want them to do. Whether it is buying a product that you are selling or simply completing a task that you want them to complete, you will be able to influence them to do so.

Mind control works like this…

First the person has to be in a relaxed state, you will not be able to control someone's mind if they are not relaxed. After the person is relaxed, you will be able to use the techniques that you will learn later on in the book on them. You will also learn how to get people to relax around you.

You can use mind control online in a blog post or in social media. Take this for example:

If I wanted you to **buy** something for instance, if I was selling **my** car, but I knew you were not really interested so I changed the subject to my new **book** I am writing. **Now** look back on the paragraph you just read, what do you find? If I had not told you to look back on the paragraph you would have had no idea what I did but you realize that the words "buy my book now" are all in bold. These four words will stand out in your mind even if you do not consciously know it, causing you to think that you should buy my book. You can use this for all sorts of things when it comes to social media or internet marketing.

When using mind control on someone, you want to make sure that you do all of the thinking for them, do not tell them that they should think it over. The techniques will be discussed in later chapters, but the way it works is that by doing all of the thinking for them you are able to make them believe whatever it is that you want them to.

Mind control works by convincing someone to do something that they have no ethical or moral problems with doing. For instance, let's say you are going to buy a house and you want the seller to drop the price by 25,000 dollars. You can use mind control to get them to do so. On the other hand, you cannot use mind control to get them to give you the house for free. This would go against their wants and needs.

The fact is that you cannot use mind control to get someone to do what they really are not open to doing in the first place.

When using mind control there are a few things that you have to do first in order to prepare the person. First, you must make the person perceive that you like them that you genuinely have an interest in them and you are concerned about what is important to them. Everyone wants to be liked, noticed, an accepted, when you compliment people and show them that you accept who they are, you are using a very powerful method of getting them to like you. Then you need to make them think that you are just like them. Many times the manipulator will talk about things that have happened to them in their lives that relate to the things that have happened to the "victim". Even making up things so that the person feels as if the manipulator is letting their guard down and opening up to them. This is a great step toward strengthening the bond between the "victim" and manipulator. After you have gotten the person to like you, you will have to convince them that their secrets are safe with you. Because you are sharing intimate details about your life (even if they are not true) with the victim it becomes much easier for them to let their guard down and discuss their personal issues with you. This can take a little bit of time but most people will open up fairly quickly. Finally you will have to make them believe that you are the perfect lover, friend, or companion for them. You will make them believe that you accept them for who they are and that there is nothing you would change about them. You highlight the things that the two of you have in common and build a strong reputation for yourself in the mind of the "victim". They will begin to believe that your relationship is different and special in some way.

This will open them up to trusting you and feeling comfortable enough around you that you will be able to use mind control on them. It all depends on how you are perceived by the person you are trying to use mind control on. The trick of mind control is making the "victim" think that the one doing the controlling is a friend and someone who has their best interests at heart. This will cause the person being manipulated to actually be a willing participant because they feel like they are being helped in some way and they think that they are making their own decisions.

All of this is normal for building a relationship, the only difference is that you as the manipulator are not interested in building a relationship with the person and are only interested with what you can gain. This relationship is a false one that is usually built on lies. Another reason why this is not a normal relationship is because it does not last once you as the manipulator have reached your desired outcome for the relationship, it is pushed aside and forgotten about therefore the manipulator has no further use for the person and discards them.

When you begin using mind control, you want to make sure that you start off small. This means that you are to start off with a small request something that is easy for the person that you are using mind control on to do. You do not want to start out by asking someone for a large sum of money or for them to do a huge favor for you. You will be able to do this later when you have developed your skills further but in the beginning keep your requests small and easy to perform.

Mind control works by planting small seeds into the person's subconscious. These seeds will begin to grow over time and you will be able to control more and more of the person's thoughts, behaviors, and actions. You will also be able to cause a loss of memory, or cause someone to desire something.

Mind control works in the same way that social influence works, this is when you are continually influenced by those around you, it shapes who you are in the moment and who you will become in the future. Social influence is what determines what brands are popular, how people talk, and how people act. Social influence is very similar to mind control but mind control is a very invasive form of influence so it requires the subject to be dependent on the person who is trying to control them. This is why it is so successfully used on people who do not have many friends, people who are going through a divorce, or who have been recently divorced, and those who are leaving home for the first time in their lives. These people do not have many if any other people to turn to they become dependent on the person who is trying to control them.

Much like social influence, mind control must be used each and every day on the subject. You have to ensure that they must believe that the controller is the only person they can turn to and the only person that they can trust. Being in constant contact with the subject will allow the controller to gain more and more control over the subject, and as each day passes the subject will become more and more dependent on the controller.

There are four basic steps that have to be taken when trying to control someone's mind. The first thing that you have to do is identify your target. Once you have identified your target you must make sure they become aware of you. This is called the physical layer of mind control. So you will request their attention by placing yourself close to them, they will grant you the attention that you are asking for and then you will gain access to them. After you have gained access, you can more on to the logical layer of mind control. This is where you use the attention you have gained in order to feed them information. You discuss what it is you want and why. The next layer of mind control is the emotional layer. In this step you cause your subject to have an emotional response to what it is you are telling them, without allowing yourself to be sucked into their emotions. You must play the part and pretend to have the correct emotional responses but not allow your emotions to become part of the situation. The final layer is called the hyper-arousal layer. This is where the fight or flight response kicks in on the subject. You can use something to make them feel vulnerable. For example, if I were a cult leader, I would start out by getting the persons attention, telling them about all that I believe in, get them to become emotionally involved in what I am telling them, and then tell them if they do not join me the will suffer some severe consequence. It is that simple.

CHAPTER 3: What are the Benefits of Using Mind Control?

Using mind control on those around you can have many benefits. You can learn how to make more sales by using mind control, get people to do whatever you want them to do, get people to give things to you, and even control how people feel about you.

By using mind control, you may be able to do things for you for free that would normally cost you money. You can get people to believe in what you say and even share it with others.

I recently watched a video online that talked about mind control, and it asked questions such as:

- Do you want a large amount of followers?
- Do you want to be treated like a god?

- Do you want people to give you all of their worldly possessions?
- Do you want people to do whatever you ask without questioning you?
- Do you want people to do whatever it takes to make you happy?
- Would you like it if people would kill for you?

Now some of these questions seem a little outrageous, not everyone who is interested in mind control is a cult leader in the making, they don't want people who will kill for them, and they don't want people to freely give them all of their worldly possessions. Most of the people who are interested in using mind control are normal people who want to learn how to use mind control in order to benefit themselves or those around them.

Ways you can benefit from using mind control:

- Get the promotion you have been asking for – you have worked for it now get what you deserve.

- Get people to buy your product or service- tapping into the market can be hard, use mind control to ensure your business is successful.

- Get people to do things for you. Keeping up with life can be hard at times. Sometimes we need a little help and we don't like paying for it, so just use mind control to get people to help you pick up the slack. Need your lawn mowed? Use mind control to get someone to do it for you.

- Get your children to mind! Yes you can even use mind control on your children to help mold them into the people that you want them to be. Can't get your kids to clean their rooms? Use mind control to get them to do whatever it is you ask of them.

•Use mind control to bring your ex back. Many of us have heard that you can't make someone love you, well guess what, that is wrong. By using mind control you can bring your ex back and make them love you.

•Get out of trouble. Next time you find yourself getting pulled over for speeding simply use mind control to get yourself out of the ticket.

As you can see, using mind control can benefit you in many ways. As long as you are not using unethical techniques such as torture or sleep deprivation to get what you want.

The benefits of using mind control over those around you are basically being able to get whatever you want from whom ever you want whenever you want it.

How you can use mind control to benefit those around you:

Did you know that by using mind control you can help those around you? For example, do you know anyone who is really smart but just can't get it together because of some mental block? Did you know that through mind control you can take that block away and allow them to really be their true self?

For example, you have a friend who is very artistic, but because of their low self-confidence they do not show many people their paintings. You can use mind control on the person to make them open up and display their paintings, you can help them sell their art by using mind control on them. If you were to use mind control in this situation, then you have just helped your friend become successful by using mind control on them.

Helping those around you is the greatest benefit to using mind control. Helping them to become what they truly want to be without causing harm to them is what mind control is all about. This is the part of mind control that most people do not understand. When people think about mind control they think about causing others harm, not about bringing peace and joy to the lives of others.

The cons of using mind control:

You may look at the benefit of being able to get people to do whatever you want, whenever you want and think that it would be wonderful, but before ever trying anything new you must not only look at the pros, but you must also look at the cons.

•It may be tempting to abuse the power that you have when you are using mind control. If you are the kind of person who knows that they will continue to take and take until there is nothing left there is a high chance that you will abuse your power. Also, if you are a person who has a history of abusing power that has been given to them than you may want to reconsider using mind control on anyone.

•You can become suspicious of everyone around you. When you begin using mind control techniques, there is a chance that you will be unable to trust anyone in your own life for fear that they are using the same techniques on you. You will find it harder to make friends with new people and can very easily become isolated.

•Using mind control can come back to haunt you. If those around you find out that you are using mind control techniques you may be left with no one in your life. Think about how you would feel if you found out that one of your friends was using mind control, even if it was not on you. Would you ever be able to trust that person again? Would you want to continue allowing that person to be part of your life?

•If you become angry at the person you are using mind control on what will you do? Using mind control takes a lot of discipline and wisdom. You cannot allow yourself to cause harm to someone while using mind control just because you are upset with them at that time.

•You may become obsessed with using mind control and lose your own identity along the way. Many people become so power hungry when they use mind control that they do not think about the person that they are becoming until it is too late. They are only thinking about what they can gain. Then when they realize what they have become it seems far too late to ever go back to the person that they once were.

•The final con that you have to think about is if using mind control on someone goes against your moral or ethical beliefs. Do you feel that you have the right to decide for someone what actions they will take in their own lives?

Mind control is something that has many benefits if it is used properly but it is also something that has been abused by many people. I has caused harm to thousands of people and to their families all around the world. If you really want to benefit from using mind control than you have to be able to ensure that you do not lose control of yourself. You have to focus on getting what you want without taking advantage of your subjects, and you have to ensure that you do not allow mind control to take you over. It is a personal decision to use mind control but it is not a decision that should be taken lightly. You should spend time weighing the pros and cons, think about how you will ensure that you do not become a victim of mind control by allowing it to take over your life, and seriously think about if you could become one of those people who ends up abusing the power that comes along with being able to use mind control.

If you feel that you can handle all of the power that comes with using mind control and you will be able to keep control of yourself when using it than you should continue on, but if you think that there is even the slightest chance that you could cause harm to those around you by using mind control, you need to stop now and do some self-work before continuing on and beginning to use mind control.

If it is all about trying to get a group of people to follow or worship you than the techniques that are taught in this book are not for you. On the other hand, if you want to use mind control in order to help yourself or those around you than you will learn all you need to in the following chapters. Mind control is not always about getting people to drink the purple Kool-Aid, it can be about helping them get what they really want and helping you be successful in life.

CHAPTER 4: Beginners Techniques

In this chapter I want to discuss beginner's techniques for using mind control. As I discussed earlier, you have to ensure that the person you are trying to use mind control on trusts you and feels relaxed around you. After you have accomplished this you may then begin using the techniques I will discuss in this chapter.

Let's start with how you use your voice. When most people talk, they finish a sentence by using a higher pitched tone than what they normally talk in. If you want to persuade someone to do what you want them to do, when you talk to them you should finish each sentence with a lower tone that what you were stating the rest of the sentence in. This gives their brain the impression that you are demanding them to do what you are asking of them. When you use a higher tone at the end of a sentence the brain instead perceives it as a question. So if you are "asking" someone if they would buy your product or whatever you are wanting of them and you finish the sentence with a lower tone of your voice, they still think you are asking a question but the subconscious mind takes it as a demand. This changes the way people think about the "question" you asked them. Using a lower tone at the end of your sentences will cause the person to do whatever it is that you are asking of them. You should practice this before you use it because when you naturally speak, you use a higher tone at the end of the sentence and if you try to chance this while speaking to a person and don't practice it, it will sound awkward and will not work.

The next thing you need to think about is what you are saying. You need to use terms that get the brain working. Using terms such as "what if", "think about", "what would happen" these will open up the persons mind to your suggestions and will allow you to tell them why they should do what you are asking of them.

When you are getting to know the person, they will reveal all of their secrets to you, then when you begin using mind control on them you are in a sense going to use it against them. For example if the person confides in you that they only buy certain things because they love the way others look at them when they see them with that specific product. They have confided in you what makes them feel good. So if you are trying to sell them something, you can say something like, "Imagine how jealous all those people will be that do not have the chance to get this, think about how they will look at you and wish they were you."

This makes the person you are trying to use mind control on think about how good it feels to them when others look at the things they have, they enjoy making others jealous and you are using that to sell your product. This is called anchoring, which means simply that you take the memories of good feelings and project them on to whatever it is that you want the person to do. You have anchored their mind to the good feelings they had and projecting them onto your product.

You can also use sexual attraction to help use mind control on those around you. The way this works it that you build up a lot of sexual tension between you and the person you want to control. You make them think that they will have the chance to be with you. They will get to a point where they feel like they are "falling in love" with you and this is where you can begin to control them using other techniques. This makes mind control very easy on these people because they already want to do whatever they can do please you.

When you use this technique, you want to keep the person sexually aroused but not give into them. You want to withhold yourself from them so that they will do whatever it is you want them to thinking that they will in turn get to have some type of physical contact with you.

Pacing is the next beginner's technique that I would like to talk about. This is where you hypnotize someone during everyday conversation by mirroring their actions, body language, and the way they talk. You want to make sure that you do not do it in a way that is apparent to them but in a way that only the subconscious mind picks up on. This will once again cause them to trust you and make them think that you are just like them. They will become attracted to you as a person because they will see themselves in you.

After you have become successful at mirroring their actions, you will begin the process of bring them to an altered state of consciousness. In order to do this you will need them to relax and breathe deeply, you can accomplish this by having them tell you a story about a happy relaxing time in their life. They do not have to reach a deep hypnotic trance in order for you to complete the hypnosis, as long as they are in a relaxed state it will work.

Now it is time to place the command into your conversation. For instance if the command is clean your room you would want to incorporate this into a sentence or question. You can start with asking them how often they clean their room, then you will need to keep adding a few layers to it. Ask things like, how do you feel after you clean your room, do you feel better when you clean your room, and so on. Now this may seem very simple but it is best to work with a simple command when starting out than to work with something more complex. You will work up to the more complex demands later. You want to make sure that you repeat the phrase clean your room multiple times while still keeping the person in a relaxed state.

When you begin practicing this, you want to make sure that whatever your command is can be carried out immediately. There is no point in using mind control on someone if they cannot do the action you are requesting right then. If you use pacing, you will see that after your conversation the person has the urge to go and do what you wanted them to do.

Repetition is very important when it comes to using mind control on someone, first you must be very patient and remain calm at all times. You do not want to become over baring and become angry with the person because the mind control is working slower than you would like it to. You will find that this is one of the easiest methods of mind control. The more that you repeat something, the higher the chances of you obtaining it. This does not mean that you continually repeat the same words or phrases over and over, this will only annoy the people around you. You simply discuss it in different ways over a period of time. When you repeat yourself, you cause a hypnotic impact on the mind.

So let's go back to the idea that you want your child to clean their room. You will repeat this multiple times throughout the day using terms such as: You need to clean your room. When are you going to clean your room? I need you to clean your room. Clean your room. How long until you go clean your room? You will continue doing this until it is in the child's mind that they need to go clean their room that they cannot think of anything else until they have cleaned their room.

Make the person you are using mind control on perceive you as figure of authority. You can do this by using the fact that you are successful at your job, or that you have a degree, or just by using the way you dress to cause them to perceive you as an authority figure. People are often subconsciously intimidated by authority and they are more willing to do what those who are in a position of authority want them to do. This is why you see so many people following cult leaders, the person has convinced them that they are in a position of authority and people naturally want to please those that hold those positions.

The last technique I want to talk about in this chapter is giving a reason. Give the person you are trying to use mind control on a reason that they should do what you are asking. When you give people a reason, they are much more inclined to do what you need them to do. For example, if you need someone to mow your lawn and you are talking the person you want to use mind control on, you can say something like, "I really need someone to mow my lawn for me because I am so busy with the kids, work, and my job that I barely have time to sleep. It would help me so much if I could find someone to mow my lawn." This has given them a reason which is to help you because you are overwhelmed with all that you have to do. This is a very effective technique and I can tell you from firsthand experience it works very well. It can pretty much be used on anyone in your life, not just someone you are focusing on using mind control on. It can be used on family and friends also and they have no idea that you used the technique to get them to do what you wanted them to do.

CHAPTER 5: Advanced Techniques

In this chapter I want to discuss advanced techniques that you can utilize when using mind control. First I would like to state that it is very important that you master the techniques mentioned in the previous chapter before attempting to use any of the techniques given in this chapter. It is important that you work through each and every technique that I have already given you so that you can use the techniques I give you in this chapter to build upon your mind control skills.

First I would like to discuss the silent treatment as an advanced technique in mind control. This one may seem childish on the surface but if you look deeper it is a great technique that you can use in order to control the way someone thinks and feels. As discussed earlier when you want to control someone's mind, you want to make them feel as if they can be relaxed around you and you want them to become dependent on your friendship. Using the silent treatment may seem like it is counter intuitive but this is how it works. Once the person depends on you, they feel as if they must be in contact with you, they rely on communication with you and they may feel as if they are falling in love with you. Now if you want them to do something for you, you take that away from them. You suddenly ignore them, don't answer their texts for a day and see what happens! After you ignore them for a little while and I do stress little while, you pick up as if nothing happened. The subject will be so grateful that you are back in their life that they will do almost anything you ask of them. I stressed a little while because you don't want this to go on too long, you want them to remain in the frame of mind that they are unable to function without you being part of their life. I would not continue the silent treatment for longer than a twenty- four hour period.

Using cause and effect to control the minds of others. This one is also fairly simple but it takes a lot of practice to learn how to talk in a cause and effect manner. Let's go back to the clean your room scenario, when you use cause and effect, you will say to the subject, "You can't find your shoes (this is the cause) so you might want to clean your room."(This is the effect) Simply stating cause and effect to someone makes the feel like you are right and that they should heed your suggestion. This is just a basic example. A more manipulative and complex way to use cause and effect to control someone's mind would be if you are trying to sell your product, you could say, "It is obvious that you are an intelligent person, therefore you can understand all of the benefits that come along with the purchase of this product." The cause is that the person is intelligent, and the effect is that they understand all of the benefits they will receive. Using this in your everyday talk will ensure that you are able to use mind control to get what you want from people.

Using reverse phycology in order to control someone's mind. Many people are confused when it comes to using reverse phycology, instead of using reverse phycology, they become more of a passive aggressive. They will say something like, "I don't care if you go out with your buddies," thinking that it will stop the person from going out with their friends. In reality this does not work, it is just a way to annoy most people and you will never get anyone to do what you want if you are passive aggressive.

So let's go back to needing someone to mow your lawn. You can always say to your husband, "Hey are you going to mow the lawn?" Or you can use reverse phycology and say, "The lawn is in serious need of being mowed, so I have decided to hire a lawn service. I need you to give me money to pay them." Watch your husband jump up and mow the lawn! What this does is provides an alternative action to your husband mowing the lawn without placing any blame on him for not having it mowed. The alternative should not be one that the person would normally agree with, for this example paying for a lawn service when your husband can cut it himself. So rather than your husband being preoccupied because you are placing blame on him for not mowing the lawn all he can do is consider how much it is going to cost to hire a lawn service and how it would just be cheaper if he did it himself. This is what makes reverse phycology affective, as long as you say it like you mean it.

Staying positive is another advanced technique when it comes to using mind control. People respond better to positive motivation than they do to negative stimulation. For example, instead of threatening and yelling at someone to do what it is that you want them to do, you should reinforce the positive benefits that they will receive if they do what you want. You have to continually make them think that you have their best interest at heart and that you are simply suggesting they do what is best for them. It works in much the same way as using rewards and punishment. People will respond better to receiving a reward for a job well done than they will to being punished for not doing their best. They will work hard in order to receive the reward you are offering. The reward when it comes to mind control is to make you happy.

Planting seeds of thought. This is one of the most subtle ways you can use mind control to get people to do what you want. Take for example if you are trying to get a friend to be healthier but the problem is they are addicted to hamburgers. You can't just come out and tell them all the things that are wrong with fast food and restaurant burgers this will just get on their nerves, but you can take a more subtle approach. Next time you go out to eat with your friend and you are looking through the menu, make sure you point out how you are looking for something besides a burger because of the news report you saw about how it was processed. Next time you are not feeling well joke around that you think you are getting mad cow disease. Once you have dropped enough seeds of thought into your friends mind, they will not be able to avoid thinking about how unhealthy burgers can be for them.

Asking for more is a great advanced technique when it comes to using mind control. You may think to yourself, "How am I going to get what I want by asking for more?" The answer is simple. Let's say you are trying to get someone to donate 10 dollars to your cause, this may be a large sum of money for that person. So you will begin by telling them that most people are donating at least 25 dollars. The person doesn't want to give you 25 dollars so you tell them that you can settle for a donation of 10 dollars. This will make the person feel relieved that you are not asking them for the full 25 dollars and they will gladly hand over the 10 dollars. I have used this technique in my own life and was able to get 800 dollars out of someone. It simply went like this, I needed 1500 dollars, I called the person on the phone and explained to them why I needed the 1500 dollars. They of course said they would love to help but 1500 was just too much I then informed them that someone else had offered to give me 600 dollars and if they could only come up with the other 800 dollars then I would have what I needed. Guess what, within an hour they were at my house delivering the 800 dollars I actually needed. The idea of giving me 1500 dollars was something they could not wrap their mind around but when I dropped that amount to almost half they were more than willing to bring it to me. That is what you have to do. You need to at least ask for double what you need and then when you drop the sum, they will be more than happy to help you out.

Reframing can be used in order to control someone's mind. This is used when someone tries to give you an excuse of why they cannot do what you are asking of them. For instance, if you want someone to go out and jog with you but their excuse for not wanting to go is that it is hot. You will state their excuse in your reply to them. For example, you could say, "It is a little warm out but that will only cause us to sweat a little more which will only cause us to lose more weight!" You have to put a positive spin on their excuse and show the person how they will benefit from what they are trying to use as an excuse.

Use what motivates the subject to get them to do what you want. For example, if your subject wants to be popular and date the most attractive people than you will be able to use that against them to sell almost any type of diet, exercise program, or drug. The way you do this is that you talk about how they will be able to reach their goals of being popular and dating only the most attractive people if they buy your product. You say things like, "Imagine what it would be like to walk up to the most beautiful woman in the room knowing that she would walk out on your arm." You will make them think about how happy they would be if they bought your product.

Finally, if you are working with your subject on a day to day basis, you will be able to use several of these techniques at on time. Using more than one technique will give you better results than just using one technique at a time. You can use a few basic and a few advanced techniques at the same time on the same subject. I do advise that you learn each and every technique before you begin using multiple techniques. Take a week or two and spend it focusing on each technique this will ensure that you are successful at using mind control on your subjects.

Chapter 6: Techniques for Career & Success

"Whether you think you can, or you think you can't, you're right." - Henry Ford

There is no dream or ambition that is too big for us to think into reality. With the power of our subconscious mind, there are no glass ceilings or restrictions on what we can achieve in life. Whether you are stuck in a rut, looking for your dream job, or afraid to leave your job to start your own business, you can change your situation using the power of your subconscious mind.

Steps:

1) Vision boards

Visualize success through images. For this visualization method, make yourself a vision board to represent the success you desire to create. Use a large vanguard sheet and paste cut-outs of pictures or words that symbolize success to you. For example, you could use a posh looking office, successful entrepreneurs like Richard Branson and

Steve Jobs, or your ideal work attire. Place your vision board in a prominent place where you can look at it daily as a constant reminder of what you desire and why you want it. Essentially, the vision board acts as a creative visualization tool to influence your subconscious, take note, and transform your goals into tangible reality.

2) Write down your career and success objectives

In order to reach your destination, you need to give specific directions to your conscious and subconscious mind of what you desire. Writing down your objectives will also help you move and act toward your goals while your subconscious looks for opportunities to get what you need.

Tips:

- Set career and success goals that open the way to greater wealth and financial independence.

- Your goal should have a timeline for its fulfillment. This timeline is for your subconscious to take note and fulfill in its mysterious way.

- As your goals are met, set new ones at a higher level so that you always progress in life.

- E.g., You can set your desired income from 1 to 5 years or your net worth in 5 years.

Sample:

a) "My Career Goals"; under this, list what you wish to achieve e.g., buy a house, a new car, give to charities.

b) Write a timeline for your goal in the following way: Annual income $90,000 December 31, 2025 or $20,000,000 net value December 31, 2025.

c) Write your goals on pocket-sized flash cards that you can carry with you as a reminder.

d) Protect your intentions by not disclosing your goals, especially to other people who will dampen your dreams with their negativity, thus poisoning your subconscious beliefs.

e) Share your goals only with people who are supportive of you.

f) Look at your flash cards frequently, and let your subconscious mind help you achieve your goals

3) Positive affirmations
Position yourself toward success by declaring daily affirmations with as much feeling as possible. The crux to saying affirmations is they need to be believable in order for your subconscious to not have internal rejection. For example, if you are deep in debt and jobless, "My

new job is going to be great. My finances are improving every day" is perhaps more believable to your subconscious mind than, "I'll be a millionaire by the end of the year." Once you achieve your first goal, you can always expand to manifest higher goals. Remember, it is not our words that impact our subconscious, rather the emotions triggered by our words.

E.g.

a) "I am attracting my dream job into my life."

b) "I love my work and am very well paid for it."

c) "I am open to opportunities to receive my dream job."

d) "My dreams are manifesting into reality every day."

e) "I am manifesting my dream job."

f) "I am working in a successful company with amazing people."

g) "I only think thoughts that make me more successful."

h) "I am a magnet for success."

i) "I am creating a successful and abundant life for myself."
j) "I attract success into my life easily and effortlessly."
k) "I believe in my ability to achieve success."

Chapter 7: 7 Emotions That Harm You

"Whatever we plant in our subconscious mind and nourish with repetition and emotion will one day become a reality." - Earl Nightingale

Our subconscious mind is a powerful data bank that stores our beliefs, experiences, skills, and memories. It is also our guidance system. Every time we have an emotion, idea, or memory it communicates with our conscious mind thus influencing our actions.

As mentioned earlier, we can use our conscious mind to program our subconscious mind, but the only thoughts that have lasting impact are the ones that are backed by strong genuine emotions. Unfortunately, since our subconscious mind does not discern between positive and negative emotions, it will accept both without objection. The downside is our negative emotions are often stronger than our positive ones.

In order to harness the power of our subconscious mind, we need to first recognize and learn to manage harmful emotions that are invading our subconscious mind and working against us. If you have ever wondered why you can't seem to meet your goals, eat healthier, save more money, or lose weight, it could be hidden negative emotions that are self-sabotaging your efforts.

Have you wondered why when you feel upset or angry, your body would manifest symptoms like upset stomach, stomach ulcers or high blood pressure? This is because of our mind-body connection. Our body is responding to the way we feel, which is why we need to be aware of negative emotions that are affecting our health as well.

1) **Anger**

Did you know that repressed anger can cause a person to self-sabotage his or her success?

Case study:

Tom is a 42-year-old lawyer who feels that his work is mediocre, and his current relationship is stuck in a status quo. He would like to be made partner at his firm but lacks the motivation to push for it. He has also been dating his girlfriend for 4 years but feels unable to settle down. He doesn't know what is wrong or how to get his life unstuck and moving forward. Tom grew up with controlling parents who often steered him towards their idea of a "successful" person. They wanted him to study law instead of engineering, so Tom followed their wishes. As their only son, they expected him to be made partner at his law firm and settled down with a good wife and two children by the time he turned 40. The truth is, Tom has years of repressed anger toward his parents which he could not express outwardly. As such, his subconscious mind retaliates by self-sabotaging his career and relationship in a stalemate.

Being unable to express or resolve our anger issues can lead to us self-sabotaging our own success.

Suggestions:

- Recognize unprocessed repressed anger can affect your overall life
- Recognize your stress, tension, chronic fatigue, aggression, and sleeplessness could be results of repressed anger
- Work through your repressed anger by expressing it in a safe environment e.g., screaming into your pillow or verbalizing your anger
- Release your anger gradually so that you can move forward in life

How anger affects your health:

- It can triple your risk of stroke after an angry outburst
- The chance of a heart attack doubles after an angry outburst
- It weakens your immune system
- In Chinese medicine, anger affects liver and gallbladder health

2) **Fear**

Fear comes in many forms. Some people fear rejection or intimacy due to rejection in past bad relationships or growing up with bad childhood experiences. You might notice that some people go from one bad relationship to another by self-sabotaging their relationships whenever it reaches a certain level of intimacy, because they have a subconscious fear of eventually being rejected, neglected, or dumped. So instead, they end it first by repeating this vicious cycle of either starting fights, cheating, or becoming too clingy to drive their partner away. In other cases, they could be loving and wonderful people who always date partners that treat them poorly. Sometimes our subconscious mind remembers the fear and pain from observing our parents when we were young, leading us to act the same way as adults.

All of us have fears, be it fear of the unknown, fear of failure, fear of our own inner critics, or fear of facing pain and rejection. If you realized that you are pushing opportunities and people away because of your fears or insecurities, remind yourself that you are mature enough to work through them.

Suggestions:
- Cultivate self-awareness
- Observe patterns that are sabotaging your relationships
- Learn to communicate calmly instead of blowing up
- Identify triggers that are setting you off
- Let go of your fears caused by past experiences
- Realize that relationships are seldom smooth-running and take effort

How fear affects your health:
- Weakens your immune system
- Causes cardiovascular damage
- Causes gastrointestinal problems e.g., irritable bowel syndrome and ulcers
- Impairs memory function
- In Chinese medicine, fear affects kidney and bladder health

3) Disgust

Disgust, or self-loathing, makes us our own worst critics because we habitually berate ourselves for not meeting our own high standards. Disgust or self-loathing often have no singular cause. Sometimes it is due to low self esteem, childhood memories of neglect or unworthiness, or unconscious beliefs about being unlovable or not good enough. All this emotional baggage can lead one to have a distorted view of self, which in turn creates a ripple effect into their lives. Whatever the reason, harboring such negative emotions will eventually leak into our own life.

Case study:

Anne is a successful 31-year-old business-savvy realtor who owns her own properties. Although Anne seems successful and confident to others, secretly she has always been disgusted with her own body image. Over the years she has tried many types of weight loss programs from Atkins, to Keto, to Paleo, but nothing has really worked for her.

Growing up, Anne had always been a little chubby. Her family thought she was cute and nicknamed her "Miss Piggy". Anne did not like her nickname as it made her very self-conscious, especially among her skinny friends. Now as an adult, Anne is still struggling to lose the extra weight. Unfortunately, years of self-loathing led her to self-sabotage her own best efforts with unplanned bingeing and late-night suppers. Every time Anne would overeat, she would despise herself even more, thus perpetuating the unhealthy cycle of the yo-yo diet.

Suggestions:

- Identify the inner critic that is keeping you in a state of disgust and self-loathing
- Every time you have negative inner dialogue, question its validity
- Be compassionate with yourself
- Be willing to work on yourself
- Accept that change is a process that will take time and effort

- Be willing to accept setbacks and bad days
- Keep with it and you will start seeing yourself in a new and positive light
- Self-acceptance will lead to self-love

How disgust affects your health:
- In Chinese medicine, it affects your heart thus causing insomnia, agitation, and feelings of being stuck

4) Sadness

Sadness is an emotion that can last for minutes to years for some people. There are various forms of sadness such as grief, hopelessness, disappointment, loneliness, regret, or suffering and these could originate from:

- Impending loss e.g., a loved one is dying

- Permanent loss e.g., loss of a loved one
- Non-acceptance of an event e.g., a loved one was killed in an accident

- Non-acceptance of an outcome e.g., the doctor diagnoses you with cancer

Some people express their sadness as moodiness, isolation from others, crying, lethargy or quietness. The seriousness of one's sadness depends on the root cause and how they deal with it. Long-term sadness that is not dealt with can lead to depression. Worst-case scenario, when you cannot let go it becomes an addiction that sabotages your life, relationships, work, and even eating habits.

Case study:

Rose was head-over-heels in love with Alan and in the midst of planning her wedding when she received news that her beloved father was diagnosed with stage 4 stomach cancer. Rose postponed her wedding plans to rally around her father's recovery. But unfortunately, her father passed away after a gruelling two-month-long battle. This happened four years ago but until today, Rose could not get over the sudden death of her father. Her sadness seeped into every part of her life. In the end, she broke up with Alan and was unable to hold on to her job. Nowadays, Rose hardly socializes anymore and does the bare minimum to get by. She often cries when ruminating about the past.

There are many unavoidable events that can trigger sadness in our lives. Some events are loss-related, permanent loss or temporary setbacks, but all are stressful in and of themselves. Although we cannot prevent unfortunate events from happening, we can choose how we respond to them and how they impact our minds, wellbeing and lives.

Suggestions:

- Visualize happy memories instead of ruminating over painful memories that overwhelm you with sadness

- Remember and talk about something positive e.g., Rose can talk about her father's wonderful attributes with her mother instead of dwelling on his last days

- Make specific plans every day instead of hiding behind four walls e.g., go to the gym, socialize with colleagues after work, volunteer at the animal shelter

- Plan for something that you can look forward to e.g., concert tickets, a holiday, a birthday party for your nephew

- Adopt a different view of what happened e.g., instead of regretting that her father passed away too early, Rose could reframe her thoughts and say that her father was a good husband and father who had given them many good memories.

How sadness affects your health:
- Causes appetite changes leading to weight gain or loss

- Appetite changes can lead to unhealthy eating habits thus increasing the risk of heart disease

- Prone to chronic pain such as headaches, muscle, or joint pain.

- Prone to inflammation causing irritable bowel syndrome, arthritis, and type 2 diabetes

- In Chinese medicine, sadness affects the lungs and large intestine thus making one prone to colds, tiredness, and bowel issues

5) **Hatred**

Hatred is an intense emotion of dislike for an individual, group or even for ourselves due to:

- Being mistreated or bullied by another person

- Feelings of envy

- Contempt due to someone else being inferior or wrong

- Learned hatred from parents or friends towards other social groups

- Past mistakes

Most people also have varying degrees of self-hatred, which sometimes originate from ingrained beliefs such as being told we were unworthy, stupid, or a burden by our caretakers or teachers while growing up. If a person accepts these beliefs as truthful on a subconscious level, then it might impact their lives negatively as they emulate them.

Suggestions:

- For self-hatred, embrace and accept who you are

- Do not let other people's opinions matter more than your own

- Talk to people who can offer you support

- Surround yourself with positive people

- Create a positive environment for yourself e.g., in your home or workplace

- Avoid the person who is causing feelings of hatred

- Practice forgiveness for yourself and others

How hatred affects your health:
- Impairs the immune system

- Increase risk of heart disease, stroke and heart attacks

- In Chinese medicine, hatred affects the spleen and stomach which causes indigestion, tiredness and lethargy

6) **Greed**

Greed can be described as an intense and selfish desire for something to the extent of acquiring it in excessiveness. An example would be an excessive desire for material things like money. There is nothing wrong with desiring more wealth. It means that we can take care of our basic needs, loved ones, and enjoy the things that make life better. However, greed occurs when a person cares too much about material possessions to the point where it affects their emotional life.

There are 4 types of greed:

a) Overspending
This is the person who thinks all his wants are needs and ends up spending all their income on unnecessary stuff. An example of this would be an executive who stole money from the company he works for in order to pay off his credit card debts incurred by his lavish lifestyle.

b) Hoarding

This is the conscientious scrooge who diligently saves money which in itself is a good virtue. However, his hoarding mentality leads him to believe that he needs to constantly amass wealth to the point of being stingy and putting his needs before everyone else. For example, a friend needs money for an operation, but he refuses to lend him the money because he might not get it back.

c) Self-entitlement

Sometimes, it is not people with wealth who are greedy. Even those without money can be greedy with their warped sense of entitlement that people owe them something. For example, a person who always expects his friends to pick up the tab because they make more money than him. In a way, he is angry at his friends' success and thinks they ought to pay for him because he's underprivileged compared to them.

d) Competing

This is the kind of greed that drives a person to constantly upgrade their house or car just to keep up with the Joneses. They are driven to spend so that they can show others they are just as good or better than them.

Suggestions:

- Recognize that your mind has been conditioned to act greedily. See if you can trace its roots to your upbringing or if its self-taught because of past unfavorable circumstances.

- Learn to be content with what you have, because greed is an illusion that will never satisfy you emotionally

- Condition yourself to give even if it's something small like buying someone a cup of coffee, because not everyone is a natural giver

- Develop compassion for others

- Focus on enriching your life rather than amassing material things

- Know that you cannot bring your wealth when you die

How greed affects your health:

- In Chinese medicine, greed affects the small intestine and can lead to anxiety, insomnia and mental unrest

7) **Jealousy**
Jealousy is a negative emotion that creates feelings of insecurity, fear, and anxiety. It often arises out of our reaction to perceived threat. For example, you are jealous that your boss seems to favor your new colleague and gives him all the important tasks. In reality he is just more qualified to take on those tasks. Regardless of what causes the jealousy, it always evokes other negative emotions such as anger, sadness, resentment, and disgust. In extreme cases of jealousy, a person can be driven to commit murder or suicide.

Jealousy can come in several forms:

a) Romantic jealousy

This is a common type of jealousy where there is insecurity and distrust in the relationship. An example would be a girlfriend who feels jealous and creates a scene whenever she sees her boyfriend talking to an attractive woman.

b) Friends jealousy

This type of jealousy is when a person has an emotional attachment to their friend and feels insecure about their friendship when another person enters the equation. For example, Janice was jealous that her best friend Laura was spending more time with the new friends she made at the gym. Janice was afraid Laura would drift away because she found her group of new friends more interesting to hang out with.

c) Family jealousy

Family jealousy such as sibling rivalry is a common display of jealousy. An example would be an older child who feels neglected and less favored by the arrival of a younger sibling. This type of family jealousy can carry on well into adulthood where the siblings are constantly competing for more attention and love.

b) Workplace jealousy

Workplace jealousy normally occurs when there is a perceived lack of appreciation and acknowledgement for staff's efforts. For example, a relatively new colleague getting promoted ahead of older staff can cause jealousy and resentment among the rest.

Suggestions:

- Focus on being strong and secure in yourself

- Express how you feel instead of blowing up

- Accept your emotions and deal with it clear-headedly by going for a walk or asking for a timeout

- Dive deeper into your past if it's a recurring jealousy issue e.g., trust issues because your father cheated on your mother

- Check the facts instead of jumping to conclusions

- Learn to let go instead of wallowing in jealousy

- Focus on your positive traits and strengths instead of competing with others

How jealousy affects your health:
- In Chinese medicine, it affects your kidneys and bladder which can cause adrenal problems with symptoms such as anxiety and heart palpitations

Chapter 8: 7 Attitudes that Block Abundance

"When you realize there is nothing lacking, the whole world belongs to you."
- Lao Tzu

1) Procrastination

Procrastination is not just about being lazy, having poor time management, or failing to meet deadlines. It is our emotional reaction to what we are avoiding and dreading. For example, we avoid the uncomfortable feelings of studying for an exam by spending time playing computer games. Indefinitely putting off things for temporary relief only leads us to more stress and negative feelings later as work piles up. At the end of the day, procrastinating means we are not taking responsibility for our actions and setting ourselves up for failure instead.

Suggestions:
- Instead of waiting for the mood to strike, just start small with the easiest

task and you will be motivated to keep going
- Minimize distractions around you e.g., email and social media
- Do the right thing and think about how it will benefit your future
- Think about the consequences of consistently not acting in your best interest e.g., losing your job and thus losing your house and car because you're unable to pay the installments
- Ask for help if the reason you're procrastinating is because you don't know how to get started on a daunting task

Remember procrastination is the biggest thief of time. So stop delaying as if you have a thousand years to live, for tomorrow may never come.

2) Indecision

Indecision is the thief of opportunity because a person who consistently hesitates on making decisions tends to lose out on opportunities and wastes time. Indecision is an issue of inaction because a person cannot decide due to various reasons such as doubt, ignorance, procrastination, fear, or a wait-to-see-what-happens attitude. Often, they will say things like, "I'll think about it," or, "I need more time".

Suggestions:

- Instead of becoming paralyzed by fear, accept there is no perfect decision
- You take away the power of fear by controlling your own decisions
- The best way to grow is to learn from our bad decisions
- The more decisions you make, the more your confidence grows

Remember the biggest risk is the risk of doing nothing at all. Act, pick a path, and don't let your indecision cause opportunities to slip by.

3) **Self-judgment**

Self-judgment often means we have harsh thoughts about ourselves, and these invalidated thoughts can manifest as anger, anxiety, and depression. We think that if we judge ourselves first, then no one can judge us, thus protecting ourselves from failures, other people's rejection, and expectations.

Suggestions:

- Acknowledge you are here for a purpose and you have something to offer
- Pay attention to your negative thoughts and words
- Forgive yourself for all unkind thoughts
- Be self-compassionate and tell yourself that you are worthy
- Learn to accept compliments
- Focus on your positive traits and learn to root for yourself

4) Over-thinking

It is normal to overthink things occasionally, but a habit of overthinking as a result of anxiety could be detrimental to our lives in multiple ways:

- Imagining fearful scenarios about what could go wrong to the point of inaction
- Obsessing about everything you said or didn't say e.g., "I shouldn't have spoken up at the meeting. They probably thought I was a fool."

- Always looking for perceived dangers or problems
- A vicious cycle of dwelling on your mistakes and shortcomings

Suggestions:
- Be aware when you are wasting time overthinking something e.g., you are feeling anxious, stressed, or doubtful
- Challenge your negative thoughts instead of letting them run away
- Instead of fearing potential problems, focus on the possible solutions
- Stop waiting for the perfect moment, because waiting means you are not progressing
- Accept you can't predict the outcome, do your best and let go of the results

5) **Envy**

Being envious is normally an emotion that we won't openly admit to having. You could become envious by comparing your self-worth with another person and being unhappy about their success.

Suggestions:

- Learn to be grateful for what you have, and count your blessings
- Develop an abundance mindset, because envy comes from a perceived deficiency in your life
- Think about how it harms you when you are envious of others e.g., wasting time, creating negativity, ruining your relationships
- Turn your envy into a goal because there's nothing stopping you. e.g., work harder so that you can afford a vacation in Hawaii like your friend
- Make your own definition of success instead of living by the standards of other people

6) Scarcity mindset

Scarcity mindset is thinking that there is only one piece of cake out there, and if someone gets a large piece of cake, then it means less for everyone else. Having a scarcity mindset means our mind will always focus on fears and unfulfilled wants and needs, instead of seeing abundance and opportunities. Scarcity mindset can also cause some people to become spendthrift because they want instant gratifications of their wants and needs, before someone "takes their paycheck away".

Suggestions:

- Shift your focus from a "getting by" mentality to gratitude for what you have e.g., a roof over your head and a warm bed
- Focus on the long-term and be proactive
- Understand that someone else getting the bonus, doesn't mean there won't be enough left
- Quit comparing yourself to others

7) **Victimhood**

People with victimhood mentality think that they are powerless because life is not in their control and is out to hurt them. This kind of mentality usually results in finger pointing, pity parties, blame, and pessimism. The truth is, these people are trying to avoid responsibility for themselves and want people to feel sorry and rescue them instead.

Suggestions:
- Practice being grateful
- Explore the roots of your mistaken beliefs that are causing you suffering
- Stop blaming others
- Take self-responsibility e.g., "I am empowered to create change in my life"
- Practice random acts of kindness and service to others
- You are what you focus on, so focus on your own magnificence

Chapter 9: Ask Your Subconscious

"As you sow in your subconscious mind, so shall you reap in your body and environment." - Joseph Murphy

Did you know that your subconscious mind contains infinite knowledge, wisdom and myriads of information that will baffle your conscious mind? In fact, any problem you have right now can be solved by your subconscious mind. The only catch is how to activate and access the power of your subconscious mind to give you the answers you seek.

How to ask your subconscious:

Whether you are awake or asleep, your subconscious mind is always working. But the best time to ask your subconscious mind is when your conscious mind is not working actively e.g., sleeping, walking, lazing at the beach.

1) Muscle testing

There is a pure energy that runs through the muscles in our body. We can use muscle testing as a form of biofeedback to help us get answers from our subconscious mind. In muscle testing, things that are "no" will weaken our body, while "yes" will strengthen our body.

A simple way to do muscle testing is using a single hand muscle testing technique. Simply touch the tips of your thumb and index fingers together to form a circle. Now try to break this circle using your other hand's index finger. When you are ready ask your question. If the answer is positive you won't be able to break the circle. Likewise, if it is negative, the connection will break. Practice first by asking yourself simple questions to which you already know the answers e.g. "Is my name Robert?", "Am I a woman?"

The second method is to hold your arm straight in front of you and ask yourself a question. If the answer is yes, your arm will stay upright when you try putting pressure on it. If the answer is no, your arm will drop. You can also do this exercise by asking a friend to put pressure on your arm. Again, test this first with a few simple questions before proceeding to ask your subconscious.

2) Sleep on it

Do you notice sometimes when you try very hard to remember something e.g., somebody's name, it won't come to you? Instead it will appear out of nowhere when you are relaxing in bed? In the daytime, your conscious mind is working hard and trying to solve problems. Night is the best time to allow your subconscious to take over.

- The key is to keep repeating your question so that it becomes instilled in your conscious mind
- Your subconscious will now take note of your repeated question, as it is always observing and absorbing information
- Because you keep repeating the question, your subconscious will understand it as an important matter that needs immediate assistance

- Go to sleep and expect to receive your answer. Sometimes it comes through a dream, or when you wake up the idea will drop into your head

3) Subconscious writing
- Find a place where you can write without disturbances
- Write your question down on a piece of paper
- Without any censorship, write down all the words, thoughts, and ideas that pop into your mind regarding your question
- Keep writing even if it doesn't make sense to you
- After you have finished, do not process it yet but wait till the next day
- Review what you have written with an open mind because the solution might not be what you are expecting
- The answers might also come to you

Chapter 10: How to Reprogram Your Subconscious Mind

1) **Visualization**
- If you want to reshape the reality of your life, start by visualizing how you want your ideal life to be. Our subconscious mind's main language is emotions and images. Write a script of your ideal life and then play it like a movie in your imagination. The more detailed, vivid, and emotional you make it, the more your subconscious will think it is real because it cannot tell the difference. Remember the subconscious is your captive audience. You can transfer your ideas from your conscious imagination to your subconscious to make success happen for you. Do your visualization for 10 to 15 minutes daily.
- For visualization you can also use a vision board, which is covered in Chapter 9.

2) **Affirmations**

The trick to saying affirmations that work and can program your subconscious mind is confidence and perceived truth. Simply put, although our subconscious does not know the difference between real or fantasy, our affirmations should not raise internal objections because it is too farfetched. For example, if you are currently broke and unemployed, it might be a stretch for your subconscious to believe the affirmation "I'm going to be a billionaire by this December" as compared to "The ideal job is already mine. My finances are improving every day."

- Write affirmations that have corresponding feelings, focus on the positive, and have no opposing views.

- Face a mirror, take a deep breath and speak your affirmation a few times in the morning, noon, and evening. When saying your affirmation, focus on the meaning and feeling of your words.

- Another method is to write your affirmation several times on a piece of paper daily.
- Repetition and feelings are the key to reinforcing affirmations to your subconscious.

3) Listening to brainwaves audio program
Neuroscientists have discovered that different types of brain waves can influence our creativity, habits, behavior, thoughts, and moods.

There are 5 types of brain waves:

a) Beta brain waves are associated with our waking consciousness and are important for our state of alertness, logic, and critical reasoning.

b) Alpha brain waves are present in deep relaxation, meditation, or dreaming states. This is also the optimal brain wave when we need to program our subconscious mind for success as it is when our imagination and visualization are at their peak.

c) Theta brain waves are present during light sleep, REM sleep, and meditation.

These are also optimal waves for mind programming, vivid visualization, creativity, and insight.

d) Delta brain waves are the slowest brainwaves that happen during deep dreamless sleep and transcendental meditation. During these brain waves, our body is healing and regenerating.

e) Gamma brain waves are the fastest brainwaves which are associated with high-level processing and insight.

For subconscious programming, you can use either alpha or theta brain waves to help you while you are doing your visualization work. There are many apps and online audio programs that you can download such as Brain Waves - Binaural Beats, Brainwave Tuner Lite, Binality, edenBeats for Android and iPhone users.

4) Hypnosis

Typically, in hypnosis, a qualified hypnotist will put you in a relaxed and suggestible state before programming positive and empowering messages into your subconscious mind. Alternatively, you can opt for self-hypnosis by listening to pre-recorded audio programs or learn from online courses available at websites like udemy.com

Chapter 11: THE STRUCTURE

Your subconscious mind is a construct of thoughts, feelings, experiences, and memories which are assimilated and stored into a complex structure which is constantly growing and evolving every second of every day.

Every learned habit, talent, or capability is downloaded and becomes second nature running on autopilot. Over the centuries this inner power has been evolving, from tiny one-celled microorganisms, up through plant life into more complex animal vehicles. Each stage providing valuable education for this power to assimilate the intricate processes of digestion, circulation, and other bodily functions, until it is capable of possessing the physical body of a human being.

Humans with marked disabilities or ailments from birth are tell tale signs of subconscious minds which may not be fully proficient yet in their evolution to be managing a human body in full vigour and harmony.

This mind that never sleeps, recording every impression, thought and image, is highly amenable in its nature. It builds its structure based on what you feed it through your experiences on the physical plane. By feeding I am referring to everything you are downloading on a daily basis: images, sounds, thoughts, feelings.

Being blind to this entire process as you grow up, you are no doubt being guided by a higher power or human over soul which directs your life to experience the things necessary to your evolution, so that you may be tempered and better fit to fulfil your purpose in the universal body of which you are a cell. This may be called God, Mother Nature, or Universal Intelligence. Either way there is a higher guiding power directing the lives of every creature within its grasp, and if you look back in your life you may see signs of its intelligent design. Experiences you needed to have which opened new doors for you. Experiences, which made you who you are today and have provided you with a purpose in life that you are passionate about. Your life is an endless adventure of experiences, which are constantly adding to or detracting from your subconscious bank of memory or character.

Once you are awakened you realize you are capable of enhancing this educating or evolutionary process by the use of your conscious mind and will power upon the highly amenable nature of the subconscious mind.

Once you have been awakened to your destiny or universal purpose, it then becomes your duty to assist nature by engaging in the conscious evolution of your being. This is done via the conscious programming and reprogramming of your subconscious structure.

Through strict discipline and a daily regiment you are to add to your inner power structure all the tools and experiences it needs to fulfil your purpose.

You must learn to take control of your own evolutionary process and assist Mother Nature in the development of your talents and abilities.

THE FILTER

Your conscious mind is the filter of your physical experience. You decide how every experience effects your well being, or how it is added to your memory bank. For all experiences of which you feel to have no control, you must learn to spin them in a positive manner no matter how painful or negative they may seem. It is imperative that they are assimilated in a harmonious fashion. Like attracts like, and the more harmony you can build within your structure, the more drawing power it has over your life to attract more harmonious conditions.

The opposite is also true and is how many of the race ignorantly operate, complaining about negative conditions and allowing them to be downloaded in a manner which is not beneficial to their structure. This then draws more disharmonies and the cycle continues until it is broken by positive reinforcement and the utilization of a different outlook on life situations.

You must take every experience as a learning opportunity and to see the jewel of it. Find the benefit. Reap the reward. This is mental alchemy. You must find the gold within the dross, or you must create that precious metal from the heap of what others might term to be a garbage experience. When you develop this mentality over time every situation becomes a winning situation. You not only create this habit that runs on autopilot, but you develop a success consciousness by continually adding more positive tools to your structure. You become Midas, every experience you touch turns to gold added to your subconscious mind. This step is imperative and can be achieved by rigorously examining every situation that arises in your life. Accepting them as they come, and having faith that the higher guiding intelligence is doing its job, pushing you along in your evolutionary journey.

Everything is a forward march, the universe spins in one direction, and that direction is forward. Learn to tune into this forward movement and understand that life has existed for eons and will continue to exist indefinitely. This forward movement is entirely devoted to your development and benefit, provided you are moving along and contributing to your cause.

Painful experiences can prove to be very powerful energy or fuel centres within your subconscious mind which propel you into directions of action, passion, and creation towards your destiny. These painful experiences are assets which are to be handled with extreme care, and must be conditioned to ensure they are assimilated in the most positive fashion possible.

You must learn and develop the habit of only accepting positive experiences into the store bank of your subconscious mind by rigorously examining every situation that arises in its educating and golden light.

TRANSMUTATION

Surely your subconscious mind is full of painful and garbage experiences that have coloured your outlook on life as you have grown. These memories and ideas are then responsible for your current living situation, good or bad. Those with great childhoods and successful supporting parents tend to be successful and accomplished, where as children from broken homes tend to have a tougher time succeeding, more often than not because they've never had the support necessary, nor the beneficial experiences necessary downloaded within their subconscious minds which contribute to and are responsible for success in life.

Whether you are successful in business, relationships, finances, etc is all highly dependant upon what you have experienced in these areas on your evolutionary journey through life. Negative painful experiences tend to draw more negative painful experiences, and one may find a hard time finding a fulfilling relationship if all they've had during their lifetime is countless troubled encounters.

In order to change your fortune in these areas, you need to delve deep into the store bank of memory and find these experiences that may have contributed to your current lack, or difficulty. Once they have been identified, they need to be re-assimilated in a positive beneficial fashion. One may simply do this by examining in it a new light, and finding the jewel of it, realizing it was necessary and good for you. Once you change your mind on it, your memory of it changes. It no longer is living and acting as the negative painful experience it was when it was downloaded, it has now been picked up, polished and laid down with pride and care. This discards all disharmonious energy associated with this experience and then becomes a power point within your subconscious structure.

The trouble is in finding these past experiences, and then in identifying them as causes to your current situation.

The transformation of them is the easy part provided you are consistent and rigorous with their examination, and have faith in a higher guiding intelligence which provided that jewel to you for a REASON.

The mind tends to create blocks to the real troublesome events you have experienced in life, masking them, essentially protecting yourself from experiencing them over again. These blocks simply hide it from your conscious memory, but this painful energy is still highly energized and operating from your subconscious structure attracting into your life experiences of similar vibration.

Psychotherapists around the world work with their patients to disassemble these blocks and release that painful energy which may be causing countless complexes in the personality and character of the patient.

You must learn to be your own psychotherapist, or you may work with professionals who may be able to help identify these areas for you.

You must identify and neutralize all negative painful experiences that have been downloaded into your subconscious structure.

INNER MAGNETISM

The subconscious mind directs the processes of your bodily functions through a psychokinetic effect, similar to a puppet on strings. These strings are lines of force which connect your body to your subconscious mind and which are severed up on death. These strings can be intercepted by other minds that reside on the subconscious plane, and this tends to happen to individuals under the influence of alcohol and narcotics. They become someone else, or may do things that are contrary to their nature later regretting and wondering how that came about. Being "under the influence" is no mere play of words.

Let this be a warning that if the personality survives the grave, there may be individuals wandering aimlessly within this plane looking to merely satisfy base gratifications that they miss from their earthly experience. It is important you protect yourself, and do not open the doors to such influence.

The subconscious mind also has a psychokinetic effect upon the people, circumstances, and events that come into your life. Your inner power is a linked to the higher guiding intelligence and can communicate its wants, needs, and fancies to it, miraculously bringing about these situations in your physical life. It operates on the scientific law of chemical affinity, or more popularly known as the law of attraction.

Like attracts like, what you tend to digest and store within your store bank you tend to experience more of. "For he that has, to him shall be given". Now I pray you are beginning to understand the importance of the contents of your subconscious mind, and the role it is playing in your life. As the old saying goes, garbage in, garbage out. You need to create a rich mental diet of images, phrases, and feelings that begin to build up the desires you have into your inner reservoir, which will then act with its psychokinetic effect to bring them into your life.

Your subconscious mind possesses a psychokinetic power that is responsible for bringing into your life the people, places, experiences, and successes you tell it to.

FUSION OF ENERGIES

Let me take this chance now to remind you that everyone you know possesses a subconscious construct that they are feeding daily. By associating with people on the physical plane you are also associating with their inner energy on the subconscious plane. If they are on a poor mental diet of lack, disease, lust, greed, anger, apathy, you too will be exposed to those energies in one way or another. If you are involved sexually with someone of a poor mental diet, the effect is dire. Intimate interaction fuses these energies together and if their construct possesses energy centres of which you are not aware they can prove to affect you in multiple ways. Sex is not to be taken lightly.

Marriage is the fusion of these energies into a unified structure whose magnetic power is greatly intensified. Two souls united become stronger than one. By choosing the incorrect mate to exchange vows with, usually a decision based on sexual attraction alone, you essentially are mixing two compounds together which do not fuse well and have the potential to be creating a highly toxic chemical compound. Many times these compounds combust into highly dramatic episodes and circumstances. Pain is the outcome. The number one problem with the race currently is their lack of knowledge of the fusion of energies and the importance of choosing the correct mate for marriage.

Avoid negative people like the plague. Remove slack, lazy, unmotivated individuals from your circle. Limit contact with negative family members as much as possible. This digital era has proven to be difficult for young people to escape the grasp of a negative parent. In the days gone, once you left home you were free. Now a days with phone, text, email, social media, and video conferencing there is no real easy way to sever those ties. Become busy, driven, and unavailable. Give your time and attention in small titbits and make those titbits highly valuable. Have a second number, an alternate email, a separate social account. Filter anyone and everyone who might be carrying an aura of negativity into your nets and limit their access to you. They will thank you one day when you are successful and are able to assist them in ways you cannot currently. Do not feel guilt. Believe in yourself and know doing the right thing can sometimes be difficult.

Be wise with whom you mingle. Remove negative influences from your life.

Chapter 12: What's With The Subconscious Mind?

First, in case you did not know, I'd like to inform you that the mind is made up of two parts; the conscious mind and the subconscious. I know reading subconscious and conscious mind is a bit too sciency for some of us and we don't understand that shit.

For that reason, I'll just call the conscious mind Jimmy and the subconscious mind John – I hope you can relate. If not, just call them whatever you want; maybe names of food or girls – whatever resonates with you.

The important thing is that you get the concept of what we are talking about here.

Master and servant relationship

One is the master and the other is the servant but mostly they are always fighting. John thinks the other's ideas and beliefs are full of crap and can never be – and it proves it by drawing back on stored data. The problem is, Jimmy is the one that gave that data; it gave everything to that spineless moron.

You see, John is created to be subjective. He has no power to reason or think independently. The sucker relies on Jimmy; this is where it gets all the information and commands. Its job is to act.

The gardener and the garden

For better understanding, we can view Jimmy as the gardener who plants seeds. John is the garden or fertile soil where the seeds germinate. Now they can be at logger heads of who is more important than who, but we know that no seeds can germinate without a garden and also that there can be no garden without plants. We know they all matter but...

The quality of the soil determines the harvest. So the subconscious determines the quality of your life by shaping your beliefs and perceptions. All this determines what you achieve and what you become. It can make you the biggest fucked up loser or non-achiever there is or you can put it under you and kick ass to change your life for the better.

So, let's view John as the enemy that you need to capture and make work for you – trust me, he is such a badass. To capture an enemy, you need to know how they operate so you can execute a plan to conquer. Let's get started;

Understanding How the Subconscious Mind (John) Works

Whether you are asleep, working, talking or walking, John is busting ass, making sure that your behavior is in sync with your emotionalized thoughts, hopes, and desires. It does not sleep a wink, even in your deepest slumber and thus it does not miss a thing. This is why you may hide your emotions, thoughts, desires and hopes but one day one time, you will sell out – your behavior will tell everybody. Have you been thinking about that beautiful colleague, admiring her hair or butt? Watch yourself! Keep it up and one day, surely you will find yourself reaching out to touch or screaming her name when you doze off in your office.

In your mental realm, it is responsible for making sure you stay in your comfort zones. It keeps you thinking and acting the same way, consistent with what you have said and done in the past. This is simply to mean that if you have been stuck in a rut entertaining unhelpful thoughts, John is here to make sure that you stay that way. He has all your thinking and acting habits stored and has memorized them such that when you try, even a little to step away from them, he pulls emergency brakes like ' hey that is not like you dumb ass' and pulls you back. This sucker will not allow you to change, not willingly. He just wants you to be the same old low-life and screw up that you have been – it's his job.

Have you experienced fear or discomfort while trying to do something that you have not done before? You could be trying to speak up in a meeting and right before you open your mouth; somehow you freeze, afraid and uncomfortable? Well, it's the same sucker at work. He is reminding you that you are that quite dormant loser you have been for the past year who worries about what everybody else will think. These feelings are psychological signs that John has been activated.

The subconscious mind is that stifled voice inside. The one that whispers and tells you that it's impossible to balance on two wheels the first time you try to ride a bicycle. It will keep at it, discouraging your attempts, reminding you of every reason why you can't. You may as well stop trying and feel that good feeling of being back to your familiar place.

Where does it get all these ideas from?

As we mentioned before, John gets all his ideas from Jimmy. Remember, Jimmy's job is to define the thoughts and action within our awareness. It deals with reality; what your five senses can establish. So, it's safe to say that the ideas and beliefs John holds come from our environment (what you have been exposed to) and the society. For instance, the belief that no one will like you when you are fat may have come from something an important person; a person whose opinion you valued told you when you were 4 years old. That thought dominated you and now, 20 years later, your still fussing about how fat you look even when you are a size 2, looking malnourished. Why? Because,

Your thoughts make your reality

Every thought that you allow to dominate your mind, creates your reality, thanks to John here who is always watching, listening and recording. Regardless of what you say you want or the things you promise yourself to achieve, if there is no data to back up the fact that this is possible, you will always fail and find yourself stuck in a rut. This must be the reason why habit change is so damn hard.

All it takes is one subconscious belief that things are not going to work out because of ABC – John is surely going to give you all the reasons. You will stand on your own way to achievement of said goals and even if you start, somehow things just fuck up because you do not believe. Then the sabotage will be there to say 'I told you so, fool' in a much louder voice.

Always remember this fact; thoughts become words. The words you say then become your beliefs. What you believe in starts manifesting in your action. It won't be long before your actions become your habits. Those habits make you who you are; they define your reality.

Now how you choose to perceive your reality will determine your experience in this cold world we live in and believe me it could be fucked up as hell. But it all lies in your mind. If you have been asking 'WTF is wrong with me?', the answer lies in some lame limiting thought in your subconscious mind that you do not even know you are dragging around.

All in all, at a 'reasonable' point of view, John works to keep you safe; to keep you from doing something that you have never done just in case it hurts you. He does not realize that comfort inhibits growth. Forgive him though, he is just doing his job and always will. You just have to learn how to make him work for you instead of against you. Outsmart him and bring him under you and that person you have always admired, the life you have dreamed of will become yours regardless of the hell hole you have come from or how messed up you have been before.

You actually have a chance, to do better, to become better. You just have one job to do; make the sabotage, the whisper and 'protector' your b#tch! I'll show you how. You've come this far, don't stop reading now.

Chapter 13: Connect With Your Subconscious Mind

The way we live, most of us have never made contact with our subconscious minds (John, remember?). We don't even know if the damn thing exists! You can't blame anybody, this world is so fast paced and screwed up that we lack the time for some real important shit. Well, you had better make time for it – it can change your world.

Scientists have discovered ways that you can make contact and connect with John. We all like easy stuff but this is not going to be easy or comfortable – at least not at first. But trust me; you will want to do this as it will make your life awesome – though it may not seem so in the beginning.

Meditate

The first thing that comes to mind with a mention of meditation is the folded legs, open arms and closed eyes with a 'dead' look on your face. I don't know of anyone who admits that they like that shit. Some say it's some messed up spirit shit inherited from the east. Well, sweetie, it may be messed up, but so are you. This is one of the best ways to connect with John and I know you want to do that. Let me explain how this works.

PS: we are going to get a little sciency here.

Normally, your brain is functioning in what's known as the beta state, which is very fast. It is associated with increased alertness but also it is said to breed some rill fucked up feelings such as anger, anxiety and stress. Meditation is meant to calm down the brain and get it to function using slower patterns. They move first to the alpha then the theta and finally get to delta patterns when you go into deep meditation.

When you enter the state of meditation, the quality of your thinking rises to a higher level. You may notice thoughts popping up from the blue. That's when something you forgot about pops up.

Note that if you try to dwell on the thought or ignore it, you will get out of the meditation state. So, please do not get your feelings involved here.

The 'popping up' thoughts are neither random nor originating from the blue. They signify that the subconscious mind (John) is asserting itself into your consciousness – you are beginning to make contact! Sometimes you may notice that your mind is jumping from one line of thought to another totally unrelated area. For instance, you may experience a thought about your upcoming presentation at the office and the next one becomes about your childhood.

It is important to note that the subconscious does not guess around the data it holds. It has a very good memory and nothing it brings up is circumstantial. If you look closely, you will find that the things you that come to your mind have a connection that the conscious mind has not established yet. Do not try to make connections then, just let your thoughts bubble. With practice, your conscious mind will learn how to become a spectator to your thoughts; Jimmy watching John. This is when you finally make good contact with your subconscious. As a spectator, Jimmy does not judge or dwell on anything; he just watches. The thoughts pass through, you get to experience the feelings but you do not stop, not even once to check what they mean or what they don't.

This will help you. Thoughts dominate your mind because you let yourself dwell on them and the feelings they stir. Through meditation, you take away their power to dominate; this is how you may finally come up with a solution to dilemmas or problems that have been screwing up your life.

Lets refer to the thought examples we used before; you may be afraid to speak in public and suffering low self-esteem. You have tried to change but the moment you try to speak, you get so terrified. Well, maybe you think you are this way because you were created a dumbass loser who cannot express themselves. In meditation, when thoughts of your failed speaking attempts come, you feel afraid and then the brain switches to when you were a child. There must be a connection. Perhaps somebody fucked up your esteem while you were a child. It could have been an important person to you who shut you up in public. That's when you learnt that your opinion does not matter. See, your conscious mind did not know that! Now you can be able to solve your issues, right?

Note

You may be feeling some kind of way about meditation because of the images of 'posed' people you have seen and probably think you cannot do that shit. Good news! You do not have to. All you need is a quiet place, away from distractions – you might want to keep the dogs and kids away. Then sit in a comfortable posture but not that you can sleep in. Meditation has a way of making you too relaxed; it's easy to get carried away in slumber.

Also, it's not easy to quite that chattering brain of yours. You cannot have good focus on your thoughts first, so start with observing your breath. Put some headphones on to quite the noise and listen to meditation music. Start with 5 minutes then work your way up as you get the hang of it. Eventually, it will be calm enough in there to watch thoughts.

Listen to that little voice inside of you; your instinct

We love to say, 'I heard something telling me…' do you know what that 'thing' is? It's your instinct dumbass. It is there to guide you. But how many times have we ignored this thing because it seems to come in to sabotage when we are trying to have fun and throw caution to the wind. It isn't spoiling the moment for you; its purpose is to prevent you from fucking up. But that bubble head of yours does not listen does it?

Your subconscious mind speaks through your instincts. Sometimes you may be facing a challenge or having a dilemma and some thought clicks in your mind in a split second, and you have this feeling that it's the right decision. That's John telling you what's right and based on how he knows you, he is very accurate many times. When you learn to listen to this voice, you learn to connect with your subconscious mind and communicate with him.

Engage and tap into your creativity

This sucker John (we are referring to the subconscious mind remember?) has an aversion for words – he leaves those for Jimmy. Many times, John prefers to speak in images, sounds and music. This is why your creative side really encourages him to surface.

This is why you will find that people express themselves through art, music, poetry or any creation that makes them feel like they have 'vented' what they feel deep inside. For this reason, whenever you feel like say singing or writing an emotional song, just go for it. Don't go and think that's its dumb to write your emotions on paper. Helping yourself is more important than that little pride of yours. Plus nobody cares whether you write them, sing or howl them. Just pay attention to that urge as it could be a sign that some emotionalized thoughts are disturbing you and that's why John is surfacing them for you to let out.

When you feel like drawing, draw. Whatever you do, nurture your creativity and don't base your creations on what others want; learn to not give a f*ck about what people say or think. What matters is what you want. This helps you come alive and to live more authentically and in close contact with the subconscious mind (John).

Now that you have met John, you can start making him work for you. The sucker is no fool though, that's why you have got to be very tactical. Let me teach you some tactics.

Chapter 14: How To Make The Subconscious Mind Work For You

The human mind, especially the subconscious part has great powers than most people have tapped. I know you have read many things about the power of the mind yet even with this information, many people do not care about riding on this b#tch to greatness. They chose to live and let life pass them by, letting the mind control them, screwing up their lives – mind you, that mind of yours has the power to screw you up or make you great. What makes the difference? What you feed it; what you plant in the garden – your subconscious.

You can distort your reality by changing the things you plant in your mental garden. This is to mean you have complete control of your mind and you can train it to think different. You can make it think in a way that creates a path for you to become awesome and attract success.

Tweaking The Subconscious Mind

It is possible to unlearn things even dated back to your childhood; yes, it's possible to rub off your subconscious of the things that it holds that have been screwing you. Don't start wondering how the hell you are going to delete memories or beliefs you have been holding for years. Heck there no way in the world you can do that!

Maybe you still hold the widely traded belief that the human mind structure cannot be changed after a certain period of childhood. That fact changed years ago as some scientists found out that the mind remains 'plastic'. It can be altered by factors such as the environment and what you feed it among other factors.

So, yes, you may not be able to delete the information on your mind's 'hard drive; the subconscious. But you can change your perception of them; you can make them have different meanings.

Let's look at some super awesome strategies to help tweak your subconscious and make it work for you;

Identify the thoughts that are f#cking you up

Don't pretend like you don't know them; those thoughts that are always sabotaging your progress. You want to start a business and then thoughts of how impossible it is, because of competitors, huge amount of capital need, you are not cut out to be a business person blah blah blah…you know them better.

If you tune into your thoughts, you can agree with me that they do not just hang loose with no support. They are backed up by some emotion. For instance, the type of thoughts in our example above, are driven by the emotion of fear. To break the self-defeating, self-sabotaging line of thought, you must cut it from the core; tackle the fucked up emotions.

How do you handle this?

Understand how your subconscious is controlling your emotion

The subconscious likes to ride on emotions. It is important to know that the little sucker loves to kick in when you are down; for instance when you are feeling uncertain or scared out of your wits by what your conscious mind can perceive.

If you want to control the subconscious, you have to understand how it is sitting on and controlling your emotions. Of course, it is using the stored data of what you have seen, heard or said and referring to past experiences. You cannot erase the data, what you can do is take away the power to use emotions by detaching your emotions from where they are not needed – the subconscious will have nothing to ride on! Emotions won't do anything for your work and tasks. They need you to work your ass off and to start now! Stop bringing those little suckers into everything you do; they will sabotage you big time!

Learn to practice specific visualization

They tell you to practice positive visualization. That's right; you need to see good things coming to you. But we are adding specific to it. Why? Because waking up and visualizing that your day will go well is so general, your subconscious will not even know what you mean. It does not even provide direction for your thoughts. Chatting with your crush all day could be 'your day going well' but in the end, when all that fire and butterflies have settled down, where will you be? Those kinds of things are responsible for your fucked up life. If you do not give direction to your thoughts and mind, they will give it to you instead – and it will not be heading to where you want to be in 5 years. What's the solution?

Give your thoughts good direction by being specific when doing your positive visualizations.

Visualizing simply means to see into the future; to perceive things that aren't as if they were. This is a very powerful technique for achieving success – and what you want. The power to do this comes from our favorite sucker here; the subconscious. Specific visualization is where you train your mind to think of and foresee situations in more specific detail. It helps you narrow down on what you need to work upon so you can act accordingly. Also, it programs the subconscious to take you in that direction.

For instance, if you visualize yourself being successful, being stinking rich and living la vida loca somewhere in an island, it is very possible you will be stuck right where you are visualizing that for the rest of your damned life. You don't even know the name of the damn island! And first what is success to you, how are you going to get stinking rich? You don't know? Keep on dreaming dreamer, you are going to be stuck there a long minute. Remember, there is a very thin line between day dreaming and fantasies and visualization.

You want success and a good, comfortable life. Here is an example of how you can visualize that;

Define what success is to you and what you want to do with your life? Is it getting a screen play you have been scribbling approved for production or getting your PhD in medicine? Visualize time, locations and actually feel the taste of champagne at the premier party or graduation. This is what I mean by being specific to the core. Visualizing your screen play being produced by that top company will start to give you some direction and mojo for taking the steps needed to get there. Also, you will notice that you will start to pay attention to and be attracted to things, people and opportunities that can help manifest your vision. (Just the same way you would really want to drive a BMW and all of a sudden you start noticing them everywhere – it's not that they have suddenly popped out of somewhere, it's just your subconscious directing you to pay attention to what you want. Those cars were there before.

Write down your specific visions and revise them every day when you get out of bed. It will ingrain them in the part of your mind with a very good memory – the subconscious. You can count on it to remind you what you ought to be when you start engaging in unhelpful and unsuccessful shit. Now it will not just do that. John (remember?) is not that nice – that spineless moron may try to sabotage you. Thank goodness he takes what is given to him; you can train him how to stick to your specific visualizations which will help you create specific goals. The next step will help you get it into his thick skull;

Make affirmative statements to support your choices/decisions

The thoughts and actions that you put in your schedule every waking day are what trains your subconscious how to be. In case you have entertained dumb thoughts and actions before, you should know that a vision of better will not kick the subconscious to submit immediately and direct you that way. I tell you he is a pain in all the wrong places.

He will come up with excuses of why not. However, teach him to stick to your smart decisions now. The best way would be to make affirmative statements – to back you up. For instance, if you need to read 2 chapters of a book, you can affirm this action with the following statement;

'I will read 2 chapters of XYZ book'

Repeat affirmative statements to yourself over the course of the day. This gets them ingrained in your subconscious mind. Now, do not just say it, go and take action before the end of the day. Show this damn sucker that you are serious by taking action on what you say you will do. Otherwise, he knows you are not serious and will always screw you over and show you other things that you can do, like sexting with a cute guy who is not your boyfriend, when you are supposed to be reading or doing a meaningful task.

Practice positive self talk

I know you have been thinking that you are a damn fool – and you have valid reasons why. I will not dispute that but can you put all that self-hate and judgment aside for a moment? Did you know that you have been acting like a fool because you think you are a fool – because Little Mr. John is listening, recording and programming you fools! When you are about to give your maiden performance and mutter, 'I don't think I can wow this crowd, I'm too old school' guess what dumbass, you are right! You will stand there and do like a scarecrow and bore them out of their minds! Why? Because you created that reality with your thoughts and it manifested; our Johnnie does not disappoint. Bird shit in, bird shit out – and no apologies.

Why not try something different.

Try talking to and about yourself positively, using positive affirmations. Say good things are happening or are going to happen. For instance, say, 'I am going to bring this crowd to their feet, I totally relate to them'. And do not just say it because you are supposed to; say it like you give a fuck. Don't worry about being sure. Kick that self doubt to the curb and say positive things. Even if they do not get on their feet, you did not go in there defeated. You went like a champ to win and you did! If they didn't like it, they must be dealing with some shit of theirs – which is none of your concern. The point is, even in the face of uncertainty or failure, never fall in the trap of negativity. Negative self-talk does nothing for you other than hammer the nails in your own 'failure coffin'.

Change your beliefs by actions

John (the subconscious remember?) is a smart ass fellow who will not just accept what you tell him, regardless of how much visualization and positive self-talk you do. You could tell yourself all the positive stuff and the lil fellow will be looking at you like, really are you sure about that? He's going to think you are screwing around until you actually prove you mean what you say.

How do you do that?

Take action!

If you want to change a belief that you suck at public speaking to you are good at public speaking, see it and tell it to yourself, but don't stop there. Take serious actions to make sure you nail your next speaking engagement. Read books, speak in front of a mirror; do whatever you have to do to become the best. Only then will little John start to take you seriously; only then can you change his beliefs.

Try something new and solve problems

Without muscle, your body would not be able to hold itself straight. Likewise, the mind would not be able to think straight without 'muscle'. Now the brain builds 'muscle' through neuroplasticity; a process by which it creates pathways. As they form, they alter your brain.

Now we are trying to alter your brain; to switch up on the subconscious. Trying new things and solving problems will activate neuroplasticity and help achieve the switch up. Doing something you have never done before forces the brain to stretch, creating new pathways; the more you practice that new thing or think of a solution to a problem, the more the pathways get stronger. The result; your subconscious connections are even stronger and can handle what you want to bring its way – which is tougher than it is used to.

Without new challenges, your brain stays 'old', with no new pathways and without expanding. If you took all the steps above and never tried to expand your mind, the new beliefs and ideas will have nowhere to sit. It won't be long before they wither. Same old brain will make same old screwed up sucker you have been- it has lacked the stimuli to grow.

Also, trying new things and finding solutions to some seemingly insignificant problems can give you access to information that will come in handy in the journey to pursue your dreams!

Goodwill

You wouldn't think this would have a thing to do with the state of your subconscious but it has everything to do with it.

You see, humans are pretty fucked up fellows; it's their nature to want what others have which they don't or cannot get. They are also vengeful and petty and also harbor negative feelings towards others.

Honestly, even if you sang positive affirmations all day, every day and never forgave someone who hurt you or hating on a friend who has a loving man (whilst you have a sucker who doesn't give a shit about you), you will never be able to create a positive environment in your mind. You will be so fucked up; you could find yourself switching from visualizing your meaningful goals to visualizing revenge or how to be better than someone.

Negative feelings towards others are invisible chains that hold you prisoner to a negative mental space which in turn poisons your life – negativity in mind starts to manifest in your reality.

I'm sorry, they wronged you. I'm truly sorry they seem to be better than you but I tell you to let go because those feelings aren't doing anything for you other than mess you up. Let go and you will not be a slave to your subconscious mind which is responsible for reminding you of the hurt.

You could repeat a mantra such as this everyday to achieve forgiveness and release; "I forgive and release (their name) from the animosity I have held. I freely give up my anger and pain and realize a healthy mind and body without resentment."

CHAPTER 15: How to Tell if Someone is Using Mind Control on You

Learning how to use mind control may make you begin to wonder if you could be a victim of mind control. Maybe you have noticed a few similarities in the techniques I have described and one of your relationships. If you think you are a subject of mind control, ask yourself the following questions:

1.Is there one person in your life that you seem to continually do things for?- If you find that there is one person in your life that you can just not seem to say no to no matter what they ask of you than you may be a victim of mind control.

2.Why do you continue to do things for this one person? Is it because you feel obligated or are you just trying to be nice?- Being nice to a person is one thing but if you feel like you "have" to do whatever it is this person is asking of you, chances are that you are a subject of mind control.

3.Is there any benefit to you for having the relationship that you feel could involve mind control? - Is the other person the only one who is benefitting from the relationship? Do you find that you seem to always be running around trying to make the other person happy and give them the things they desire but you are getting no benefits yourself? This is a huge sign that you are the subject of mind control.

4.How would you feel if this person suddenly disappeared from your life? – If you would feel as though your entire world is falling apart than you are probably being controlled. This is different than a husband/wife relationship. This is someone who is not married to you but seems to be the center of your entire life.

5.Does this person disappear or ignore you when you do not give into their wants? This is the technique called the silent treatment, they are trying to show you how hard your life would be without them and they are forcing you to do whatever they want in order to keep them in your life.

If you think that you are a victim of mind control, there are things that you can do in order to break free. You have already started by realizing that there is a chance someone is using mind control to get what they want from you. Here are some things you can do in order to break free of mind control.

✓ Interact and connect with others on a regular basis. This is the next step you must take if you want to break free from being a victim of mind control. This is because you have to realize that there are other people out there who do want to be your friend, there really are people who will be sincere and who will genuinely care about you without trying to control you.

✓ If you find that your mind is constantly being bombarded with thoughts that are disturbing to you and you feel have been planted by a person who is using mind control, you have to find a way to distract yourself from those thoughts. You need to find a way to keep busy and allow your mind to think for itself. When you begin to think about one of these thoughts, you need to immediately force yourself to think about something else.

✓ Do not entertain the thought that you are evil. This is just one more way that you will become susceptible to mind control. It may also be a seed that was planted in your mind in order to ensure that you comply with the demands of the person who is using mind control on you. Remind yourself that you are a loving and wonderful person whenever these thoughts enter you mind.

✓ Don't allow fear to stop you from making new friends. The person who is controlling your mind may have said things like, "No one else will ever care about you like I do," or, "You don't deserve to have friends." You have to put these thoughts out of your head no matter how hard it is and allow yourself to meet new people. Remind yourself that they only said those things because they wanted to keep you for themselves, you are such a wonderful person that they did not want to share you with anyone else.

✓ Don't worry about what others think of you, when you are around people do everything you can to be yourself and know that they will love you for who you are. When you are alone, you may have to battle with the thoughts that have been planted in your mind but you should be able to be yourself around others.

✓ Do not think that all humans are evil, evil is something that is learned and not something people are born with. You now know that there are people out there who are bad and who will try to control you, you can look for the warning signs now but you must understand not everyone is like that.

✓ Avoid alcohol and drugs, will only make it easier for you to be controlled. You need to avoid them at least until you break free of the controller in your life. You may choose to avoid them all together afterwards so you never go through this experience again but that is a personal choice.

✓ Find a good psychiatrist in order to avoid long lasting damage. You should find a good psychiatrist that you can talk to about the experience. Another alternative to this is to write a book or find a support group for people who have been through being a victim of mind control.

How can you know if you have joined a group that is using mind control? The questions that I am going to have you ask yourself are not limited to religious groups, there are many other types of groups that can and do use mind control on a regular basis so you should ask yourself the following questions to determine if in fact you have joined a group of people who may be using mind control.

1.Do you feel that no matter how hard you try, what you do is not good enough for the leader or the group? Making you feel like trying your best is a way that the groups will try to break you down, it makes you easier for them to control and you will always be trying to do better than you did before.

2.What are you motivated by? If you are motivated by the fear of not living up to the desired standards of the group or the leader the chances are very high that you have joined a group that is using mind control. You should be motivated by the purpose of the group such as saving the endanger trees or whatever their purpose if you find that you are motivated by fear, you should leave the group immediately.

3.Is questioning the group or its leaders ideas generally frowned upon? If you are not allowed to state how you feel and express your own opinions, you have probably joined a group that is under the influence of mind control.

4.Does the group that you belong to feel that they are the only ones who have the true answers? Do they think that they were chosen or are above those who are not in the group? If the group you are in thinks that they have all the answers to life and only the members of the group are the ones who are able to understand what is really going on, you need to run as fast as you can because you are not only putting yourself in the position to be a victim of mind control, you are in the middle of a cult.

5.Do the members of the group behave as if they are robots? Sometimes this will involve everyone dressing the same, wearing the same hair style, and can even be people acting exactly the same as everyone else. This is called group conformity and its sole purpose is to ensure that everyone act the same to ensure no one rebels.

6.Are you afraid to leave the group? If you find yourself in a situation where you belong to a group that you are afraid to leave because of whatever reason, you need to understand that sometimes those who use mind control, use fear as one of their techniques to control people. They may tell you that something terrible will happen to you if you leave the group because you are walking away from the truth. You have to understand this is just one of their mind control tactics and nothing bad is going to happen to you. On the other hand if you have been threatened with physical harm if you try to leave the group you do have the ability to contact local law enforcement and tell them what is going on. They will be able to remove you and help you find a safer location.

If you find that you are in a group that is using mind control on its members you have to find a way out. This may seem very difficult but you must remind yourself of all of the mental and emotional abuse that you will be subjected to if you continue to stay in such a group. You also have to understand that if you want out of the group, chances are there are others who also want out, it may just be that you taking the steps you need to take to remove this group from your life will show other members that it can be done and they can get their lives back.

Using mind control may have its benefits but when you find that you are the victim of mind control the benefits to the controller do not matter. Everyone has the right to think and act for themselves and to make the decisions that they feel are best for themselves. In this book I have given you many techniques that you can use in order to use mind control to benefit yourself but do not forget that you also need to be benefiting the subject at the same time. You don't want to be one of those people who continually take and take. If you use mind control to get something that you want, every now and then use mind control to give something back.

CHAPTER 16: Warnings About Using Mind Control

Using mind control on people obviously has some great benefits for the person who is in control. If the person who is in control is a caring person, mind control can have benefits for the subject as well, but there are some warnings you should understand before you decide to use mind control on anyone.

First you should understand that you could cause severe mental and psychological damage to the subject if you are not properly trained in using mind control techniques. This book was made to discuss several different techniques but without the proper training there is a great chance of causing permanent damage to your subject.

Another thing that can happen is that the controller may get caught up in using mind control on subjects and lose control themselves. This was briefly discussed in a previous chapter but I feel that it deserves a bit more discussion. When someone gets caught up in using mind control on others, we end up with evil cult leaders who cause groups of people to suffer at their hands.

Blocking out the subjects memories may allow them to get past some of their fears but it can also allow them to become fearless. This may cause the subject to put their life or the lives at others at risk.

Mind control may cause the subject to have severe panic attacks. This is especially true when the person is subjected to vivid imagery as a form of mind control and they are not used to such imagery.

If you use a trigger word in order to get the subject to comply they may hear the trigger word from someone else at a time when you do not want them to perform the action associated with the trigger word.

There are many things that could happen when you are using mind control on someone that could harm them or those around them, but given the fact that you are using mind control on them, the chances are that you really don't care how it could negatively affect them. What about how it could negatively affect you? If you are using mind control on people and it is found out, with enough evidence, you could be prosecuted. This is especially true if you caused them to bring harm to themselves or others, or if you caused them to give you all of their personal belongings. In court this is looked at the same as if you had walked in their house and stole everything they owned.

What will happen if people find out that you are using mind control? How will the people around you react? Chances are that they will feel whether it is true or not, that you have been using mind control on them as well. You will lose all of your friends and word will quickly get around that you have been using mind control on people. What would happen if your boss found out? He just gave you a huge raise and it comes to his attention that you are someone who uses mind control to get people to do what you want them to, I bet you lose that raise and possibly even your job even if you never used mind control on your boss at all.

Before you decide to use mind control, you have to look at all the possible outcomes. How would you feel if you caused permanent damage to one of your subjects? How would you react if those around you found out that you had the ability to use mind control on anyone you chose to? Is there a chance that you will become power hungry and turn into a vicious cult leader?

Some of these questions may seem farfetched but if you are truly considering using mind control on anyone than you must ask these types of questions. Deciding to use mind control is not a decision that should be made quickly nor should it be taken lightly. You have the knowledge that you need to control the mind of anyone in your life but the question that you should ask yourself is just because I can does it mean that I should?

If in fact you do decide to use mind control, I suggest that you start out small, use it for minor things in your life. If you find that you are able to control yourself and you do not become power hungry than you can move one to bigger things.

How will you know if you are becoming power hungry? You will know that you are becoming power hungry if you find that you are having the subject do things that could harm them. Or you will see that your subject seems to be miserable. You can also realize that you are only using mind control because you are power hungry if you find that you are never using your ability to use mind control to benefit your subject.

Chapter 17: The Difference Between the Conscious and Subconscious Mind

"The conscious mind may be compared to a fountain playing in the sun and falling back into the great subterranean pool of subconscious from which it rises." -Sigmund Freud

The conscious and subconscious mind are not separate, but rather two spheres of activity in our mind.

When you are awake, your conscious mind is the gatekeeper that is responsible for activities such as thinking, talking, reasoning and executing daily tasks. Think of consciousness as your awareness of the present moment. For example, you are reading these words right now and are aware of the aroma wafting from your coffee. If you want to calculate 2 x 6 = 12, it is your conscious mind that gives you the answer.

On the other sphere, we have the subconscious mind which stays in a dormant state as we get our work done through our conscious mind. For example, when you first learn how to drive a car, you use your conscious mind to learn how to maneuver the vehicle, push the pedal, and turn the steering wheel. Subsequently, after years of driving, you no longer need to rely on your conscious mind to drive. This is because the required information and skill have already been transferred to our subconscious mind, acting like a memory bank with unlimited storage. Thus, allowing most of us to drive, cycle, swim and speak languages on autopilot without much effort on our part.

Sigmund Freud's psychoanalytic theory of personality explains that many of our unseen and repressed feelings, emotions, desires, and memories which are kept out of our consciousness exert great influence over our behavior, feelings, judgment, urges, and basic

instincts. Freud's topographical model of the mind, which is likened to the metaphor of the iceberg, explains that we can only see the small tip of the iceberg that is above the water. This small tip only makes up 10 percent of our consciousness and represents our mental capacity of:
- Will power
- Long-term memory
- Logical thinking
- Critical thinking

Below the water, and unseen to us, is the bulk of the iceberg at 90 percent representing our subconscious mental capacity of:
- Emotions
- Beliefs
- Values
- Habits
- Intuition
- Imagination
- Protective reaction
- Long-term memory

Simply put, the most important part of our mind is the part we cannot see.

Characteristics of the conscious mind:
- Controls logical and intellectual processes
- Planning
- Decision making
- Communication through speech, writing
- Awareness of both internal and external happenings e.g., you are working on your work project and are aware it is raining outside

Characteristics of the subconscious mind:
- Control over involuntary physical functions e.g., breathing, blood circulation, digestion
- Control over our emotions e.g., fear, anxiety, sadness
- Memories
- Beliefs
- Attitudes
- Gut instincts

- Dependent at accessible information e.g., retrieve stored memory of directions in order to head home
- No awareness of internal mental functions and external happenings

In a nutshell, we can use our conscious mind to program our subconscious mind because it will obey whatever it commands without objections. The problem is most of us do not know how to program and tap into the power of our subconscious mind to achieve what we want in life. Instead of planting flowers in our garden of subconscious, we plant weeds e.g., poor habits, addictions, or self-sabotaging thoughts that make us act habitually in a manner that is below our full potential.

Chapter 18: Techniques for Health

In Chapter 2, we explained the emotions that harm our health and the mind-body connection where we feel an emotion and it activates certain neural pathways in our brain. Whether you're looking to improve a specific area of your health or your total wellbeing, the first step is to be aware of negative emotions that might be hampering your health. This step is like removing the weeds from your garden before you can start planting good seeds. The good news is once you have identified these negative emotions, you can work towards healthy subconscious programming.

- Be aware of your inner dialogue because every feeling, thought, and emotion carries energetic effects that can influence your body. For example, if you keep saying to yourself "I feel sad," it will cause stress, damage, and increase cortisol and adrenaline in your body. Imagine the long-term damage this does to your body if you do this repeatedly.

- Many diseases are manifested by our consistent toxic emotions and thoughts.

- Are you stuck in toxic emotions, such as anger or sadness, which are sending a negative feedback loop to your mind and body? Manage and take charge of your negative emotions otherwise they will control and deplete your mental strength.

- If you are currently undergoing treatment for any ailment, focus your mind on how the treatment or medication is going to help you get better. Let's say you are undergoing physical therapy for your bad knee. Instead of being passive and just going through the motions, you need to start seeing and believing that the therapy is indeed making your knee better. Use the power of your mind to expect your treatment to work.

- All sickness, be it the common flu or an incurable disease, can be reversed by releasing negative thoughts and replacing them with positive thoughts of health; healing through the mind works harmoniously with medicine.
- Our bodies respond to thoughts from our subconscious mind. Therefore, if you focus your thoughts on being healthy, you will create more health.

Steps:
- Ask for what you desire e.g., "I am healthy, and my body is perfect in every way"
- Every day, look at yourself in the mirror and say aloud your health affirmation "I am healthy, and my body is perfect in every way"
- Visualize your body in perfect health. Imagine yourself doing all the things you thought you couldn't do e.g., your bad knee prevents you from running.
- To help you visualize better, cut out pictures of healthy-looking people that

inspire you and paste it next to your mirror where you do your daily health affirmation

- Every day, try to do things that are relaxing and de-stressing to help you let go of toxic emotions and thoughts e.g., watching funny movies or playing with your children

- Be thankful and act like you already have a healthy body. If you want to accelerate your progress, keep a gratitude journal and write down three things you are grateful for before you sleep. The purpose is to let these positive thoughts sink into your subconscious and expand your awareness before you drift off to sleep.

- To keep your state of health, avoid people who are negative or focus too much on your illness

- Read (or listen) to books on health and wellbeing

- Lastly, believe and have faith that once you ask, your body is already whole.
- Suggested daily affirmations for health

E.g.

a) "I am getting stronger and healthier every day in every way."

b) "I am perfectly healthy and full of energy."

c) "I take good care of my body by eating healthy and nutritious food."

d) "I am filled with energy and physical stamina."

e) "I want wholeness and healing for my body."

f) "Healing power flows through my body in all ways."

g) "I am kind, loving and gentle to my body."

h) "I love food and food loves me back."

i) "I am at my perfect weight with a beautiful and healthy body."

Chapter 19: Techniques for Wealth

Whether you want to have more wealth for your family, start a new business, or go on holidays, it is entirely possible to manifest wealth using the power of your subconscious mind.

Steps:

- Focus on abundance thinking. Keep a daily gratitude journal and write down 1-3 things you have that you are grateful for, and then spend a few minutes instilling feelings of gratitude for them. Remember it is the feelings behind the words that carry the most weight in our subconscious. For example, you could write, "I'm grateful for my lovely home," and then you'd spend some time thinking about how wonderful it is to have a hot shower and a nice bed to sleep in.

- Your thoughts must be aligned with wealth. It's not going to work if you have habitual opposing thoughts about wealth e.g., "Things are getting too expensive. I'll never be able to retire," or "Rich people are selfish." Remember, your subconscious will not attract wealth if you keep repelling wealth with opposing thoughts. The next time these thoughts come up say, "Stop," or change your inner dialogue, "Rich people like Bill Gates give back millions to society."

- Look at the reality of your finances and identify your money blocks by writing them on a piece of paper e.g., negative thoughts about wealth, compulsive purchases, credit card debts. Review this list and write down what you are going to do about them e.g., "I'll stop buying things on credit cards."

- Write down your money objectives on a piece of paper e.g., "I want to clear my student loans in 2 years time" and review this daily

- Everyday, align yourself by repeating wealth and abundance affirmations so that they are absorbed into your subconscious.

E.g.

a) "Money is a blessing. I attract more money each day."

b) "Making money is easy for me."

c) "I am attracting wealth and succeeding in all my goals."

d) "I am a magnet for attracting wealth."

e) "I am ready to receive unlimited wealth into my life."

f) "I have a successful and abundant life."

g) "I am totally open to prosperity and abundance in my life."

h) "Money comes to me effortlessly and easily."

i) "I attract money just by thinking about abundance."

Remember, you do not need to be resigned to a life of struggle, because you alone can decide how much wealth you welcome into your life. Start to feel thankful and excited for the wealth you already have, because once your subconscious has become consumed with thoughts of abundance, more will come your way.

Chapter 20: Techniques for Relationships

Your subconscious is like gravity -always in motion and working by bringing into your life the things you focus on. Whether you choose to create your reality consciously or subconsciously, it never stops giving back more of the energy you release. Therefore, if you desire love and joy in your life, your frequencies need to vibrate in tune with what you want to manifest.

Steps:

- Let your subconscious know the type of relationship you want. Be specific and deliberate with the kinds of qualities you desire so that your subconscious will be trained to look for the best path to find it. For example, "Thank you, I'll have a partner who is family oriented, thoughtful and giving" and not "I'm single and lonely. The dating pool is too limited at my workplace. I'll never find a partner at this rate."

- Take action and work on yourself through personal transformation. Sometimes, to get what we desire we need to change ourselves first, because what we give is what we get. In other words, we need to match our vibrations with what we want to attract. For example, if you want to attract a thoughtful and giving partner, then you need to be thoughtful and giving as well. Or if you are shy and poor at making conversation, you need to learn how to better relate to others in order to have the relationship you desire. If you don't change, you won't get a different result.

- Accept who you are first. If you have low self esteem, work on yourself first otherwise you might sell yourself short and attract partners who are subpar or driven away by your insecurities. When you radiate confidence and self-assurance, you will easily attract partners who are similar and worthy of you through your subconscious.

- Don't fixate on your expectations and must-list. Be open-minded to people who are possibly a good match.

- Visualize your own story as vividly as possible so that your subconscious will be primed to look for opportunities

- If you are looking to improve an existing relationship, do not keep focusing on unmet needs and shortcomings. Practice gratitude and appreciation for the relationship, and plant good vibrations that focus on joy and connectedness.

- Change your thoughts and life by declaring affirmations with as much feeling and heart as possible.

E.g.

a) "I am loved. I accept who I am."

b) "I love myself and find love everywhere."

c) "I attract relationships that are supportive and for the highest good."
d) "My marriage is becoming stronger and more loving every day."
e) "I love and receive freely in all my relationships."
f) "I am attracting the perfect partner to live my life with."

g) "The one I love is responsive to my love, and we are coming together."

h) "I am a magnet for my soul mate."

i) "I am thankful for my caring partner who loves and supports me."

Conclusion

I do not have an opinion about where using mind control is right or wrong, but I do think that it can change your life if you decide to use it. Whether it changes your life for the better or for the worse is completely up to you and is in your control. You have to make sure you as a person are able to make the right choices when it comes to using mind control. Using mind control to make a sale, get your friend to exercise more often, or to help someone discover gifts that they never knew they had is fine. Using mind control to obtain followers and get them to do whatever you want while instilling fear in them, causing people to harm themselves or those around them, or taking everything you can get from your subject is wrong and I do not in any way endorse such behavior.

I wrote this book so people would understand how they can use mind control to benefit themselves and those around them in their daily lives. Not so people can harm their subjects and cause them to live in fear. I suggest that you take a good look at your motives before you use mind control and determine if it will help you become the person that you want to be. If you find that you want to use it to bring harm to others, I suggest you get some help and leave mind control alone. If you feel that you are a subject of mind control, please follow the advice given in this book to free yourself.

www.ingramcontent.com/pod-product-compliance
Lightning Source LLC
Chambersburg PA
CBHW050025130526
44590CB00042B/1906